SCHOLASTIC

SUMMER EXPRESS

NEW YORK • TORONTO • LONDON • AUCKLAND • SYDNEY
MEXICO CITY • NEW DELHI • HONG KONG • BUENOS AIRES

Cover design by Brian LaRossa
Cover photo by Ariel Skelley/Getty Images
Interior illustrations by Robert Alley, Abbey Carter, Maxie Chambliss, Sue Dennen, Shelley Dieterichs, Jane Dippold, Julie Durrell, Rusty Fletcher, James Hale, Mike Moran, Sherry Neidigh, Cary Pillo, Carol Tiernon, and Lynn Vineyard

ISBN-13 978-0-545-22689-9 / ISBN-10 0-545-22689-9

11 12 13 14 15 16 17 18 19 20 08 19 18 17 16 15 14

Table of Contents

Dear Parent:

Congratulations! You hold in your hands an exceptional educational tool that will give your child a head start into the coming school year.

Inside this book, you'll find one hundred practice pages that will help your child review and learn the alphabet, numbers, colors, shapes, sorting, letters and sounds, and so much more! *Summer Express* is divided into 10 weeks, with two practice pages for each day of the week, Monday through Friday. However, feel free to use the pages in any order that your child would like. Here are other features you'll find inside:

- A weekly **incentive chart** and **certificate** to motivate and reward your child for his or her efforts.
- A sheet of **colorful stickers**. There are small stickers for completing the activities each day, as well as a large sticker to reward your child for reading during the week.
- Suggestions for fun, creative **learning activities** you can do with your child each week.
- A **recommended reading list** (on page 8) of age-appropriate books that you and your child can read together throughout the summer.
- A **certificate of completion** to celebrate your child's accomplishments.

We hope you and your child will have a lot of fun as you work together to complete this workbook.

Enjoy!
The editors

Terrific Tips for Using This Book

1 Pick a good time for your child to work on the activities. You may want to do it around mid-morning after play, or early afternoon when your child is not too tired.

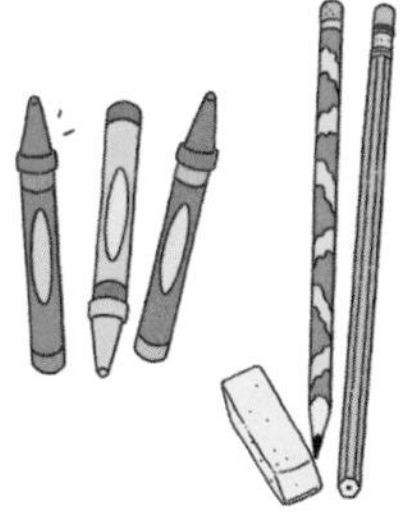

2 Make sure your child has all the supplies he or she needs, such as pencils and crayons. Set aside a special place for your child to work.

3 At the beginning of each week, discuss with your child how many minutes a day he or she would like to read. Write the goal at the top of the incentive chart for the week. (We recommend reading 5 to 10 minutes a day with your child who is entering kindergarten.)

4 To celebrate your child's accomplishments, let him or her affix stickers on the incentive chart for completing the activities each day. Reward your child's reading efforts with a bonus sticker at the end of the week as well.

5 Encourage your child to complete the worksheets, but don't force the issue. While you may want to ensure that your child succeeds, it's also important that he or she maintains a positive and relaxed attitude toward school and learning.

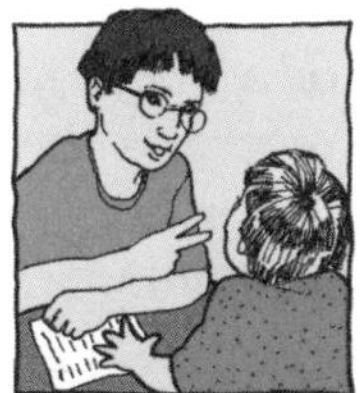

6 After you've given your child a few minutes to look over the practice pages he or she will be working on, ask your child to tell you his or her plan of action: "Tell me about what we're doing on these pages." Hearing the explanation aloud can provide you with insights into your child's thinking processes. Can he or she complete the work independently? With guidance? If your child needs support, try offering a choice about which family member might help. Giving your child a choice can help boost confidence and help him or her feel more ownership of the work to be done.

7 When your child has finished the workbook, present him or her with the certificate of completion on page 143. Feel free to frame or laminate the certificate and display it on the wall for everyone to see. Your child will be so proud!

Week-by-Week Activities

Try these quick and easy activities to enhance learning and fun!

Week 1

- Help your child write the letters of his or her first name. Together, count the number of letters in the name.
- In the park or in your backyard, lie down on the ground with your child and watch the clouds pass by. Call out shapes or figures that you see in the clouds.
- While reading the newspaper or a magazine, encourage your child to look for words that begin with the same letter as his or her name. Read the words together aloud.
- When eating colored candy, such as M&Ms, have your child count how many of each color there are in a bag.

Week 2

- While strolling through the neighborhood or running errands with your child, play "I Spy," calling out letters that you see. For example, "I spy a big, red letter *M*."
- Using gumdrops or marshmallows and toothpicks, encourage your child to build different shapes, such as triangles, squares, or rectangles.
- As your child plays jump rope, encourage him or her to chant the alphabet, one letter for each jump.
- Buy a set of magnetic letters so your child can form words on the refrigerator while you cook.

Week 3

- Invite your child to help you bake cookies and let him or her help measure the different ingredients using measuring cups and spoons.
- While reading a magazine with your child, challenge him or her to find a particular letter, such as the letter *C*, on the page and circle it.
- Help your child memorize important numbers, such as your home phone number, 911, your address, and so on.
- Let your child sit with you while you write out your grocery list or your list of things to do. This will allow your child to see authentic reasons for writing.

Week 4

- At the beach, collect seashells with your child. Later, encourage him or her to sort the shells any way he or she wants. Then ask your child to explain how he or she sorted the shells.
- Finger-trace letters on your child's palm or back and have him or her guess what letter you formed.
- Make pasta or cereal necklaces with your child to help build fine-motor skills. Provide your child with a length of yarn or lanyard and pasta or cereal with holes in the middle.
- Write each letter of your child's name (first and/or last) on a small square piece of paper, then put the pieces of paper inside an

envelope. Give the letters to your child and have him or her use the letters to create different words.

Week 5

- At the beach, use a stick to print out your child's name on the sand before the waves come in and wash it away. Then challenge your child to write a letter as many times as possible before the waves return.
- Challenge your child to guess how many steps it takes to go from the front door to your kitchen or from the bedroom to the bathroom. Then have your child walk heel-to-toe and count the number of steps. Ask your child: Do you think it would take more or fewer steps if I (or another grown-up) measured the distance the same way?
- Create riddles with your child in order to practice beginning consonant sounds. For example, "It's round and fun to play with. It begins with the *b* sound." (Ball)
- Next time your child wants to paint, offer only the three primary colors (red, blue, and yellow) and encourage your child to experiment with mixing the colors to create new ones.

Week 6

- Turn exercise time into learning time. Challenge your child to form letters with his or her body, either lying down or standing up. Some letters he or she can form are T, L, X, and Y.
- Go on a "shape hunt" with your child. Encourage him or her to look for circles, rectangles, squares, and triangles around your house or when you go for a walk.
- Provide your child with old newspapers, safety scissors, paper, and glue. Encourage him or her to cut out letters in his or her name and paste them on a sheet of paper.
- Bath time is a great time to learn about things that sink or float. Let your child bring some waterproof toys in the bath. Then ask him or her to guess whether each toy will sink or float before putting it in the water.

Week 7

- Let your child look out the window and count how many cars or people pass by in 3 to 5 minutes.
- Fill a shallow cake pan with sand or salt. Invite your child to practice tracing a letter in the sand with his or her finger.
- Play a clapping game with your child to hone his or her listening skills. Clap a simple pattern, such as clap-rest-clap, and ask your child to repeat the pattern back to you. Gradually increase the complexity of the pattern as you continue the game.
- Encourage your child to button his or her own shirt, zip his or her own zippers, and tie his or her own shoelaces to build fine-motor skills.

Week 8

- Provide your child with toothpicks or plastic straws and play dough and encourage your child to use these materials to "build" letters.
- Gather a collection of buttons and invite your child to sort the buttons by different attributes. For example, your child can sort the buttons by color, by the number of holes, and so on.
- Make a list of high-frequency words—words that appear frequently in the English language—such as, *the, to, and, a, he, I, you, it, of, in, was, said, that, she, for,* and so on. Pick a word of the day and have your child point out that word every time he or she sees it that day.
- Enlist your child's help in creating a healthy fruit kebob snack—and practice patterns. Using small wooden skewers and

different fruits, have your child make ABAB patterns (like banana, strawberry, banana, strawberry) or even ABCABC patterns (grape, banana, blueberry, grape, banana, blueberry).

Week 9

- Play "Simon Says" with your child to introduce the names of different body parts. For example, "Simon says, 'Pat your stomach'" or "Simon says, 'Touch your knees.'"
- Go on a measuring expedition with your child. Pick a nonstandard tool of measurement (such as a spoon or shoe) and measure different things at home, such as the rug, dining table, or bed.
- Give your child chalk to write letters on the sidewalk. Encourage him or her to make the letters as big as possible.
- Next time you go to the park with your child, bring some paper and crayons or pencils, and make rubbings of tree trunks, leaves, and so on.

Week 10

- Give your child coins to sort. Help him or her identify each coin and how much it is worth.
- Have your child write letters using glue and glitter. Your child can squirt glue on paper to form a letter, then sprinkle glitter on the glue. When the glue dries, your child can trace the letters he or she has formed with her finger.
- Play dice with your child to help teach or reinforce the concept of "greater than" or "less than." Each of you take a die and toss it in turn. Whoever tosses the higher number gets a point.
- While riding in a car, challenge your child to call out letters and numbers on license plates.
- To make the mini-book on pages 127–128, tear the sheet out along the perforation and cut along the dashed line. Place the two sections so the mini-book pages are in order, then staple and fold to form a book.

Books to Read

Barn Dance
by Bill Martin, Jr.

Ben's Trumpet
by Rachel Isadora

Changes, Changes
by Pat Hutchins

Click, Clack, Moo: Cows That Type
by Doreen Cronin

A Color of His Own
by Leo Lionni

Dance Away
by George Shannon

Goodnight, Gorilla
by Peggy Rathmann

Growing Colors
by Bruce McMillan

Harold and the Purple Crayon
by Crockett Johnson

How Do Dinosaurs Say Good Night?
by Jane Yolen

If You Give a Mouse a Cookie
by Laura Numeroff

Jennie's Hat
by Ezra Jack Keats

Love You Forever
by Robert Munsch

Lunch
by Denise Fleming

Market Day: A Story Told With Folk Art
by Lois Ehlert

Max Found Two Sticks
by Brian Pinkney

Of Colors and Things
by Tana Hoban

Olivia
by Ian Falconer

Piggies
by Don Wood

Planting a Rainbow
by Lois Ehlert

Three Tiny Tugboats

Trace and write.

3

Color each barge with 3 objects.

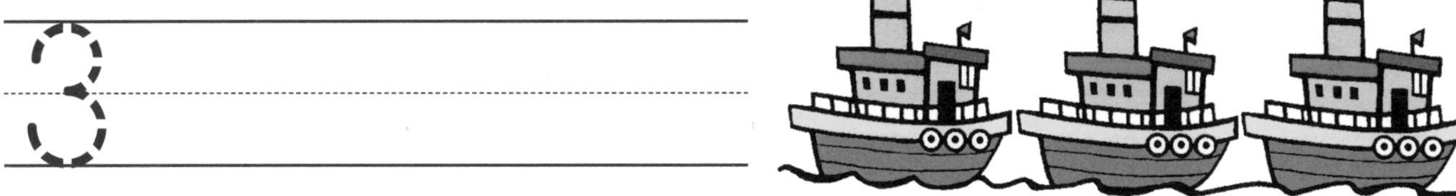

Draw 3 logs on each barge.

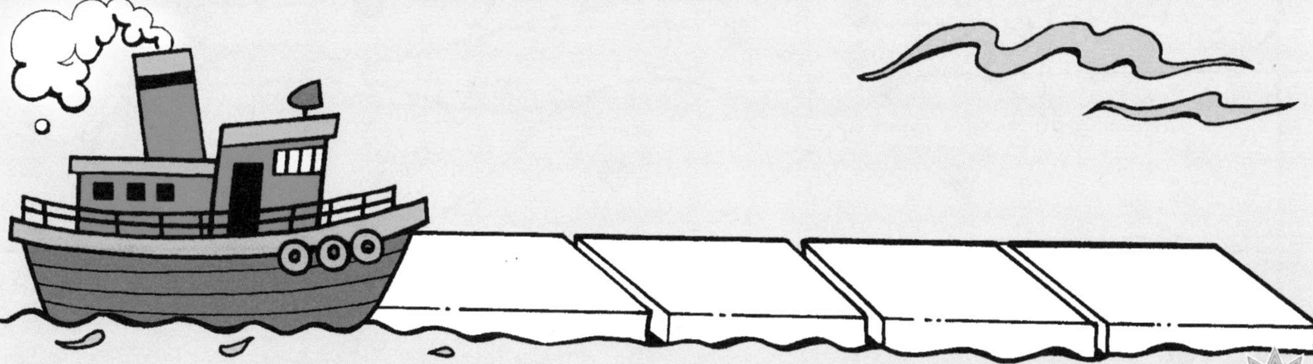

Tugboat Tow

Use the code to color the picture.

1 blue
2 brown
3 red

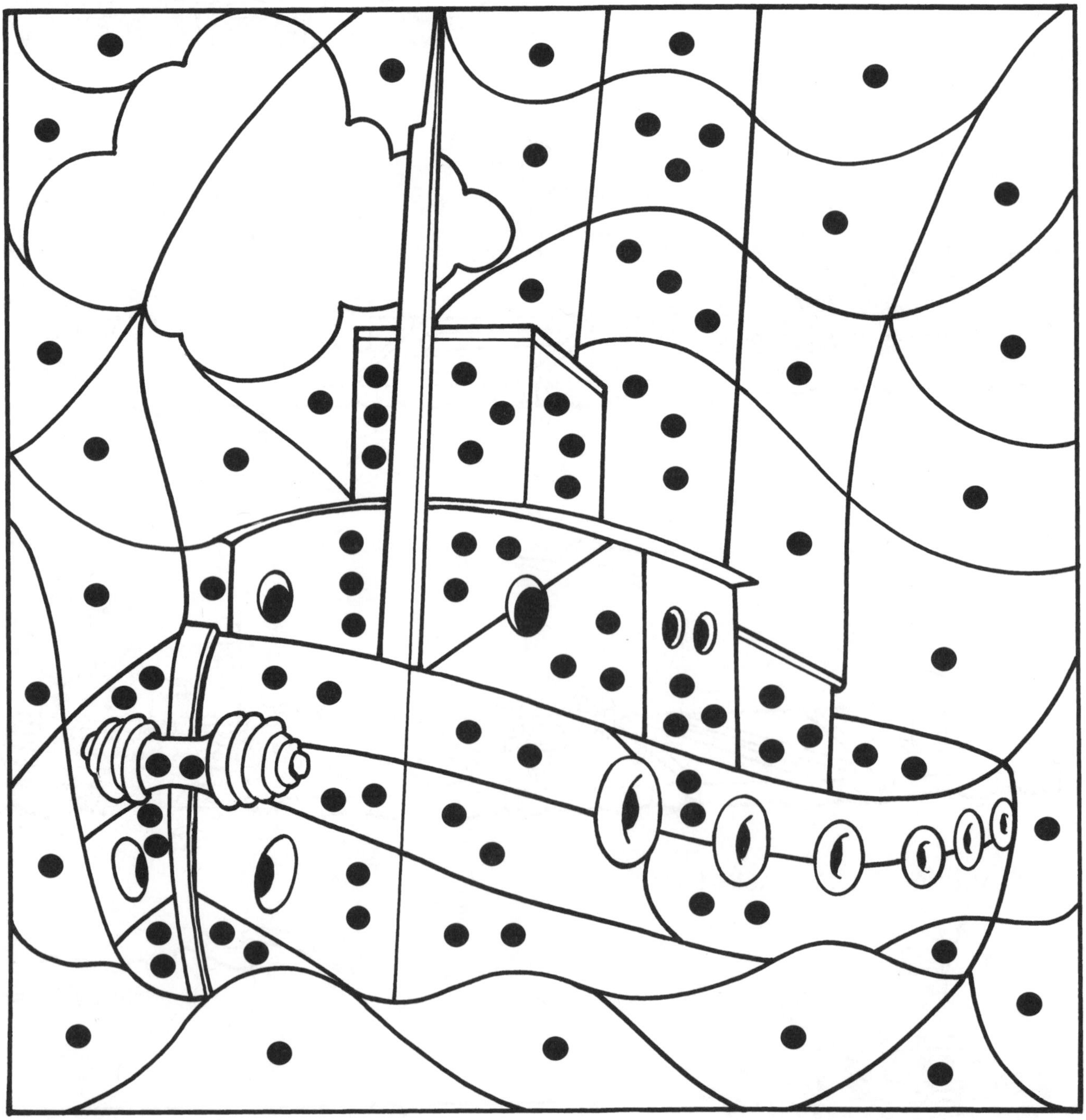

Which color did you use to color the most spaces? ____________

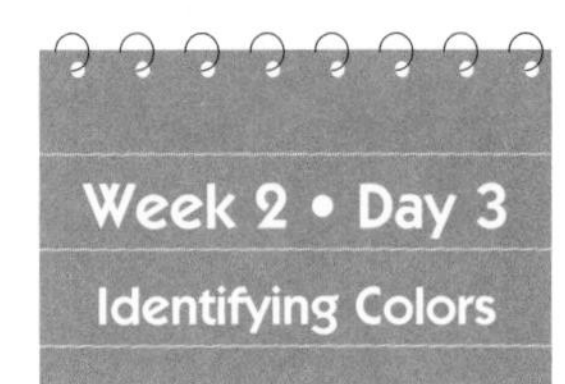

Color Train

Draw a line to match each train car to the correct object.
Color the objects with the correct color.

blue

yellow

black

red

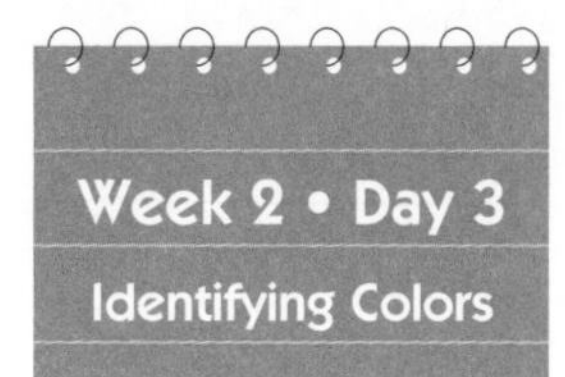

Color Train

Draw a line to match each train car to the correct object. Color the objects with the correct color.

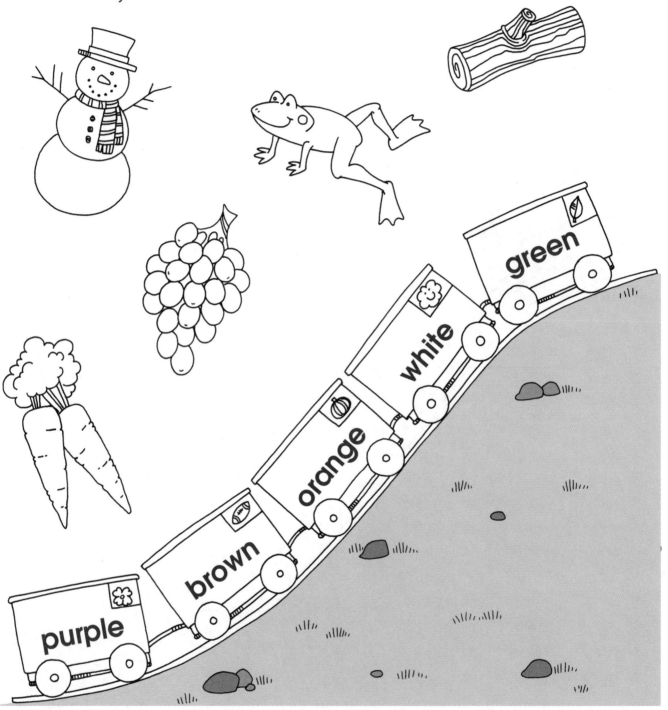

purple

brown

orange

white

green

Four Fine Firefighters

Trace and write.

4

Color each dog with 4 spots.

Climb to the Top

Count the objects on each step.
Circle the matching number.

2 3 4

3 4 5

3 4 5

2 3 4

3 4 5

FD

How many steps have 4 objects? ________

Sorting Shapes

This is a **circle** ◯. This is a **square** ☐. A square has four sides that are the same length. This is a **rectangle** ▭. A rectangle also has four sides. The opposite sides of a rectangle are the same length. This is a **triangle** △. A triangle has three sides.

Color the circles yellow.

Color the squares red.

Color the triangles green.

Color the rectangles blue.

Going to School

Find and color these things in the picture.

pencil

paper

scissors

glue

book

eraser

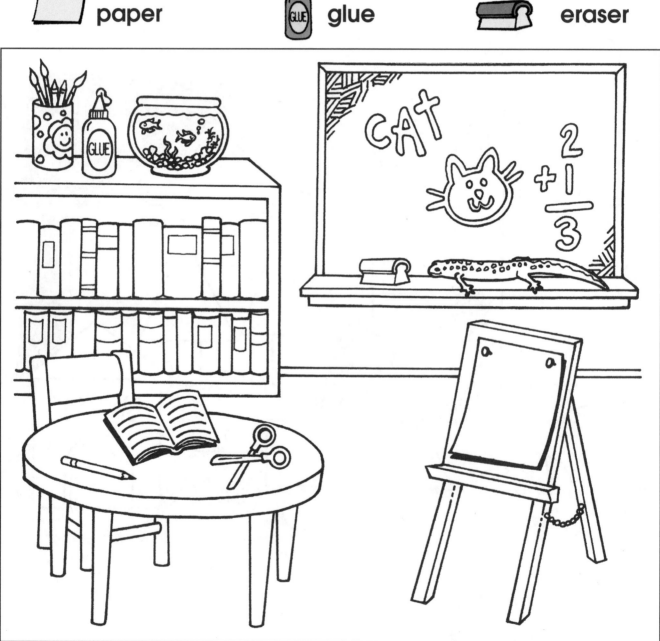

Put an X on one thing in the picture that does not belong.

_______________'s Incentive Chart: Week 3

Name Here

This week, I plan to read __________ minutes each day.

CHART YOUR PROGRESS HERE.

Week 1	Day 1	Day 2	Day 3	Day 4	Day 5
I read for...	minutes	minutes	minutes	minutes	minutes
Put a sticker to show you completed each day's work.					

Wow! You did a great job this week!

Place sticker here.

Parent or Caregiver's Signature _______________________________

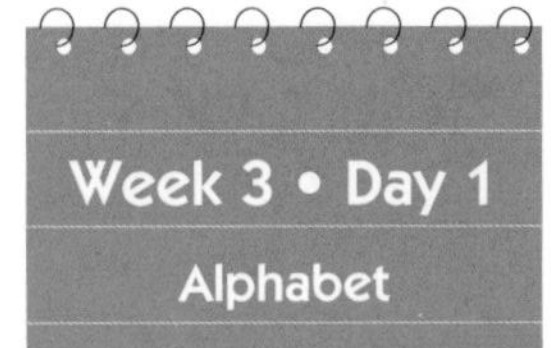

Letter A

Trace and write.

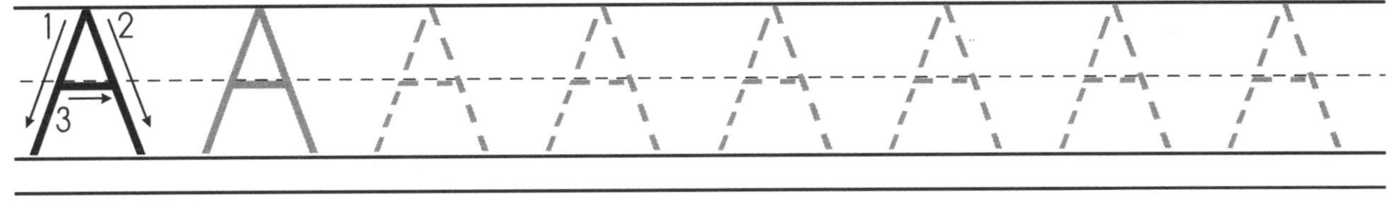

Circle every **A** and every **a**.

A E A O A O A

o e a o a a o

I found ______ A's and ______ a's.

Add a's and then read the words.

______ pple

______ lligator

______ rm

Letter B

Trace and write.

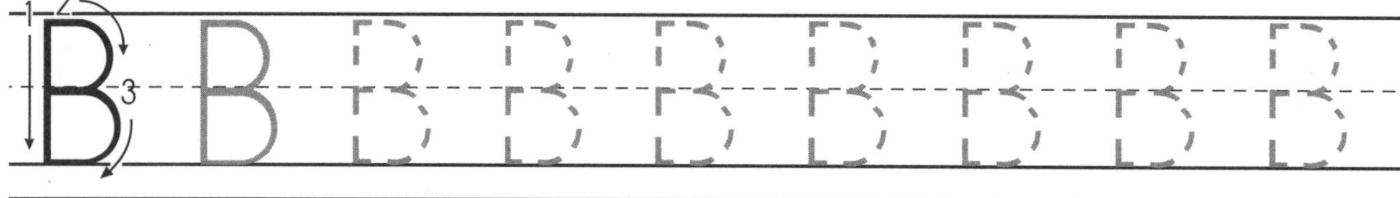

Circle every **B** and every **b**.

E	H	B	B	P	D	B
b	p	b	d	e	b	b

I found ______ B's and ______ b's.

Add b's and then read the words.

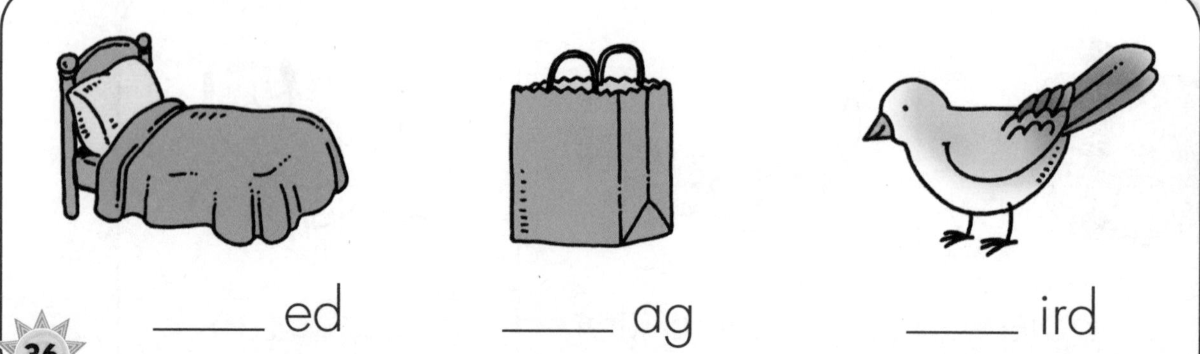

Five Friendly Frogs

Trace and write.

5

Color each lily pad with 5 flies.

Fast Frogs

Circle each rock with 5 bugs to find which frog finishes first.

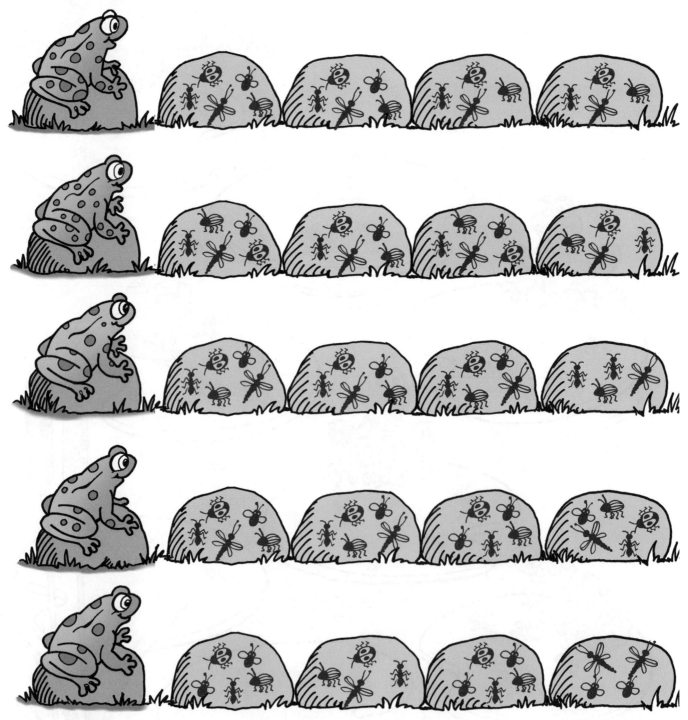

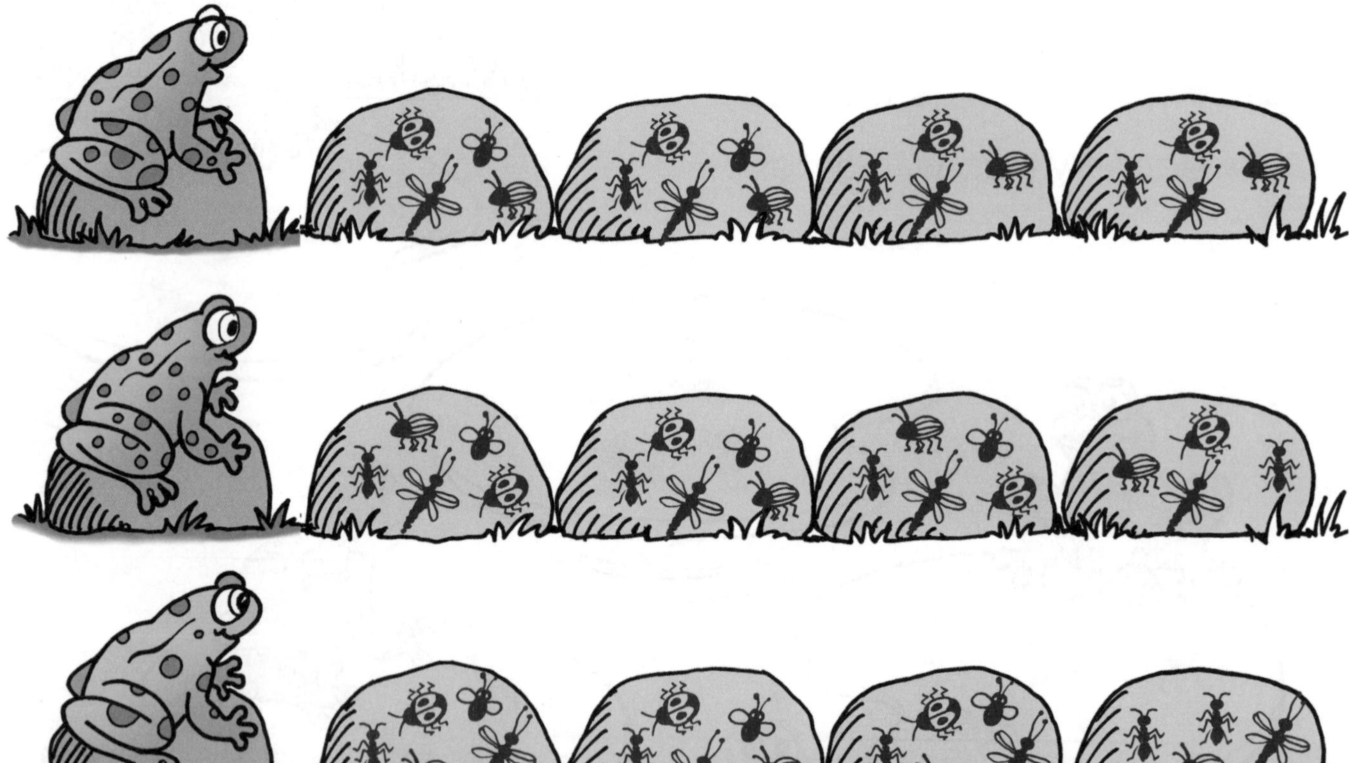

How many rocks have 5 bugs? ____________

A Shapely Castle

Color the shapes in the picture below using the code.

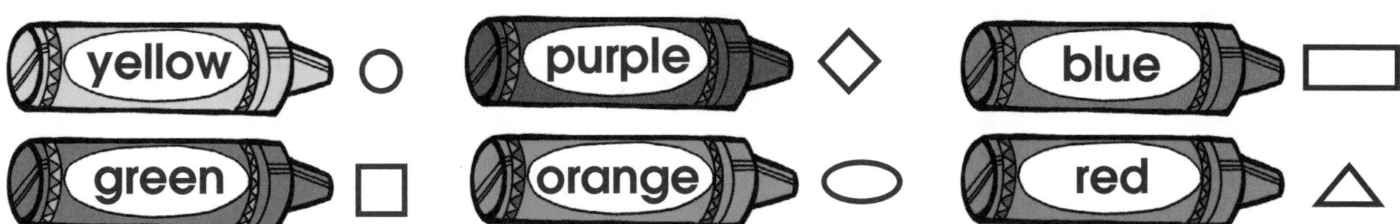

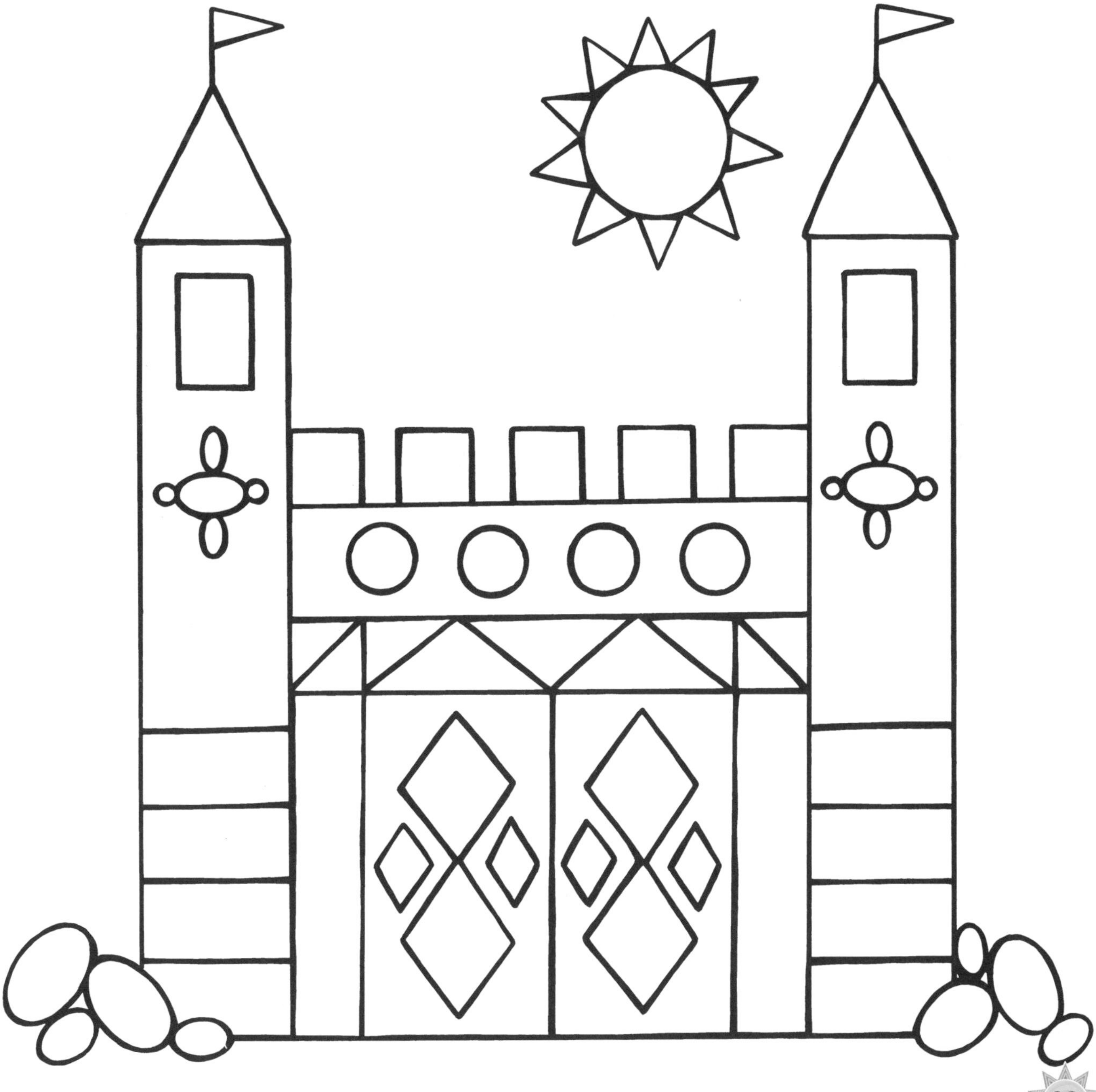

Scholastic Inc. Summer Express: Between Grades PreK & K

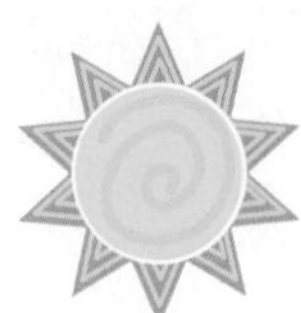

Shape Teasers

Color each shape using the code.

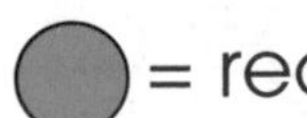 = red  = blue  = green  = yellow

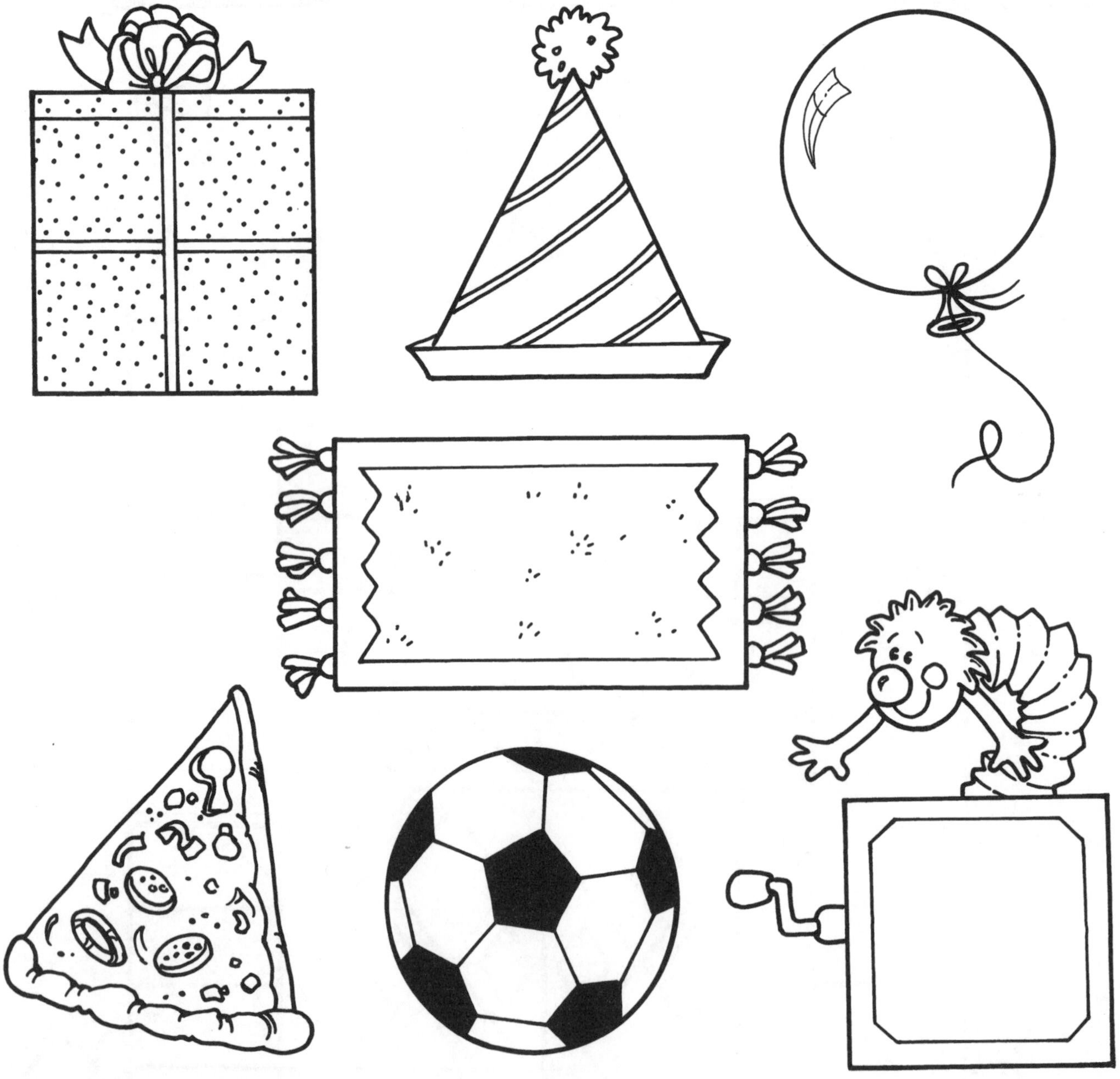

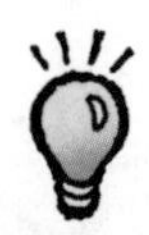

Name something else with each shape.

Six Smelly Shoes

Trace and write.

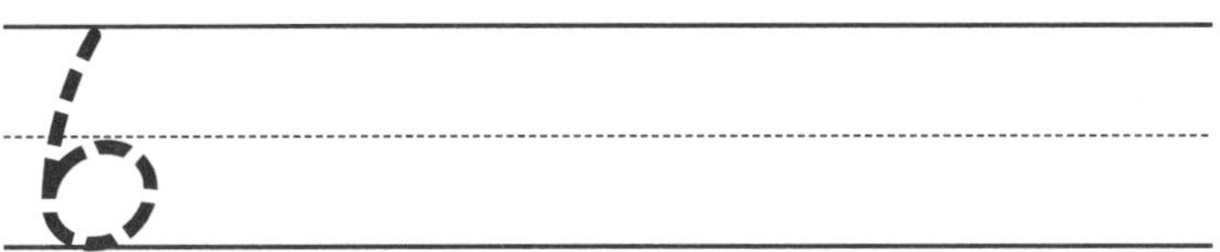

Circle 6 shoes in each box.

Draw more shoes to make 6.

Count the socks. Circle the right number. 5 6 7

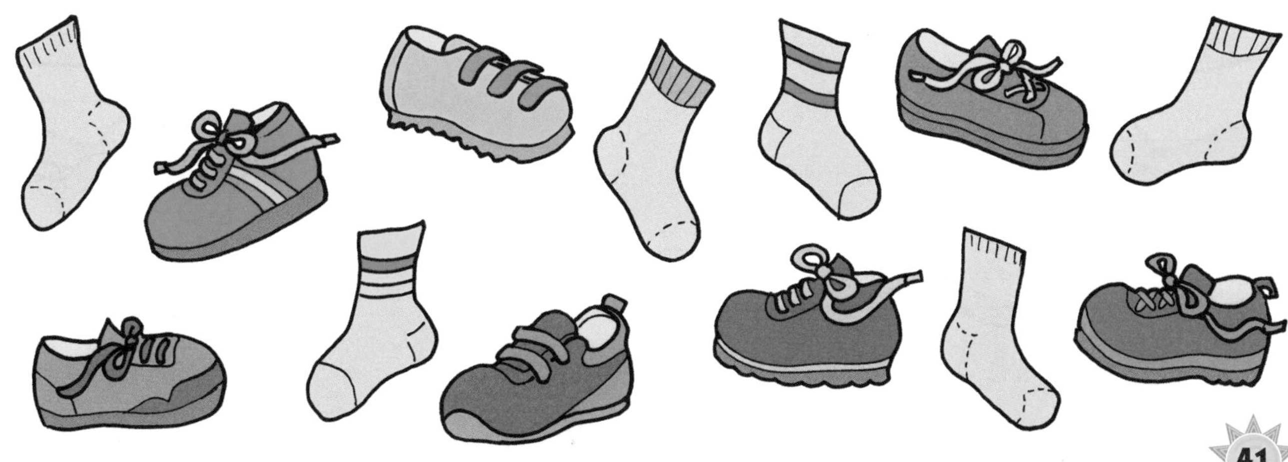

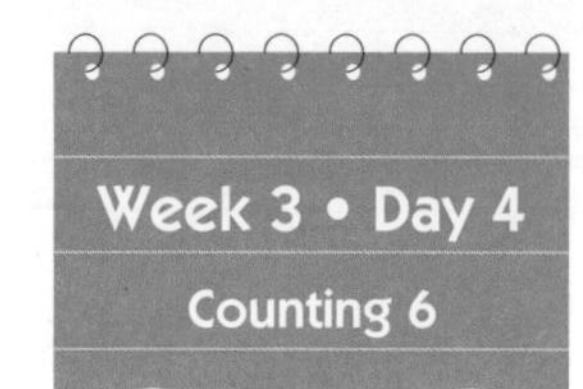

Two Make a Pair

Count the shapes on each shoe. Draw a line to the matching number.

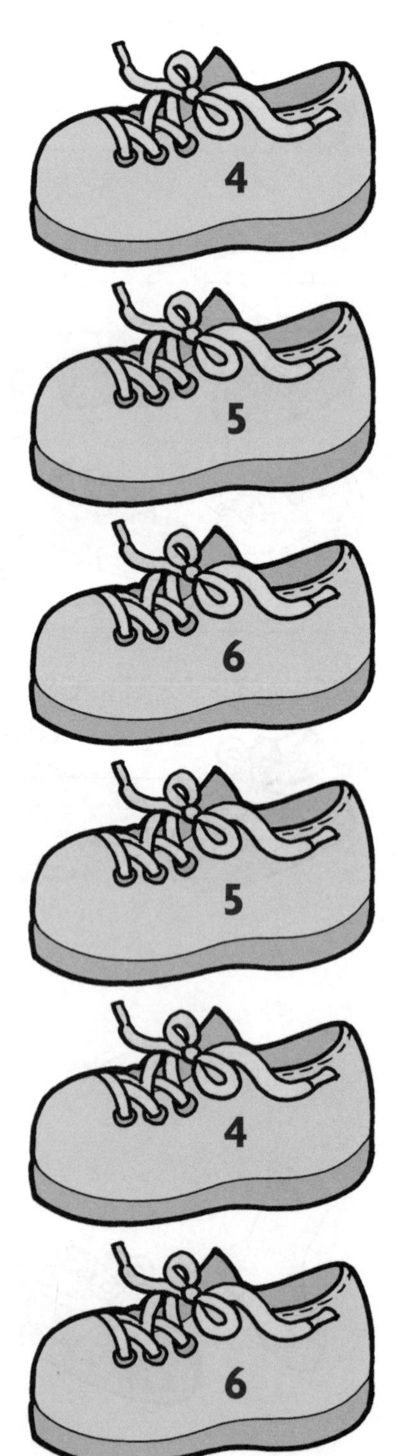

Count the shoes in your closet. How many did you count? ___________

Tricks for Treats

Count the bones each dog has. In each box, circle the dog with **less** bones.

Just the Right Size

This butterfly is **large**.  This butterfly is **small**. 

Circle the large picture on each petal.

Name two things that are larger than you.

_________________________ 's Incentive Chart: Week 4
Name Here

This week, I plan to read __________ minutes each day.

CHART YOUR PROGRESS HERE.

Week 1	Day 1	Day 2	Day 3	Day 4	Day 5
I read for...	minutes	minutes	minutes	minutes	minutes
Put a sticker to show you completed each day's work.					

Congratulations!

Wow! You did a great job this week!

Place sticker here.

Parent or Caregiver's Signature ______________________________

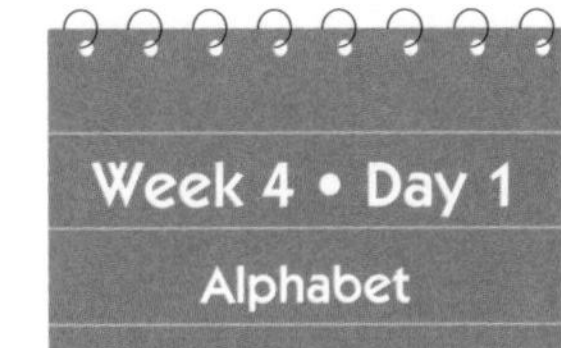

Letter C

Trace and write.

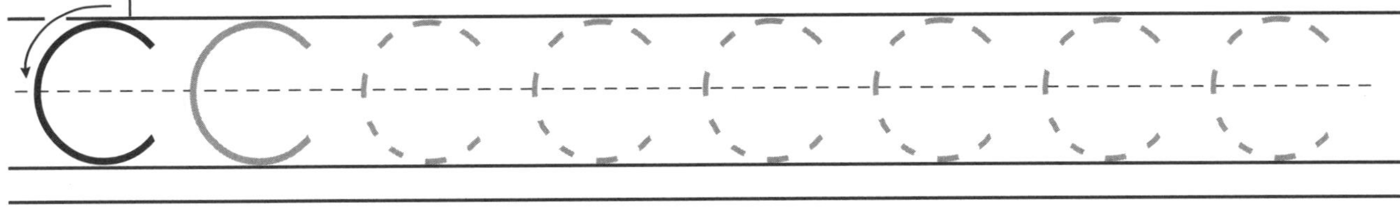

Circle every **C** and every **c**.

C C U C C D E

u c o o e c e

I found ______ C's and ______ c's.

Add c's and then read the words.

____ at

____ ar

____ ow

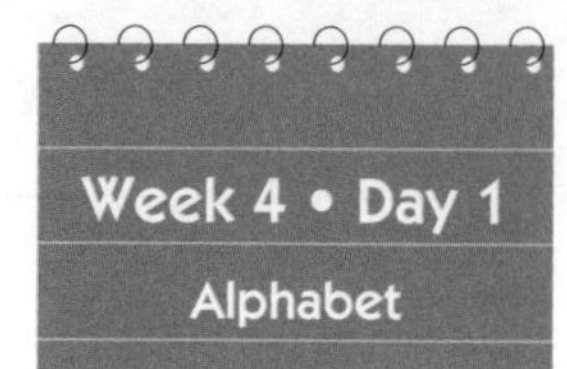

Letter D

Trace and write.

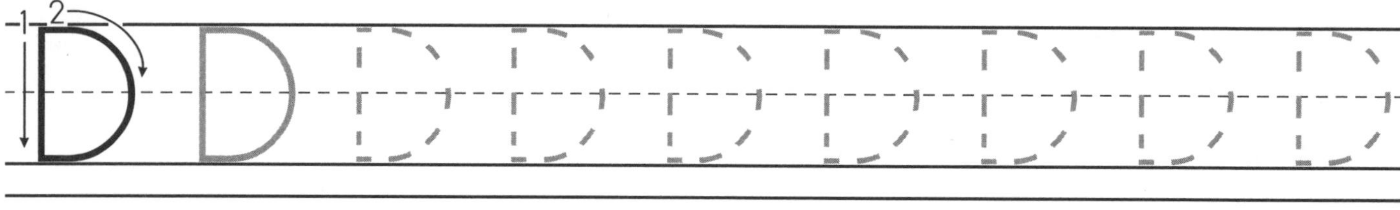

d d

Circle every **D** and every **d**.

D D O B D O D B

d p b d q d b d

I found ______ D's and ______ d's.

Add d's and then read the words.

____ uck	____ ollar	____ oor

Seven Seashells

Trace and write.

7

Color 7 shells in each box.

Seashells by the Seashore

Count each kind of shell in the picture. Write the total number next to the correct shell. Circle the shells that total 7.

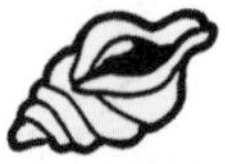

______ ______

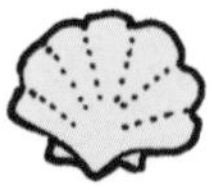

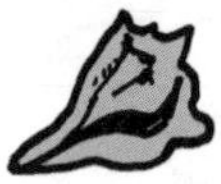

______ ______

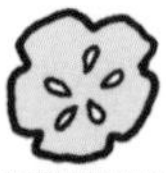

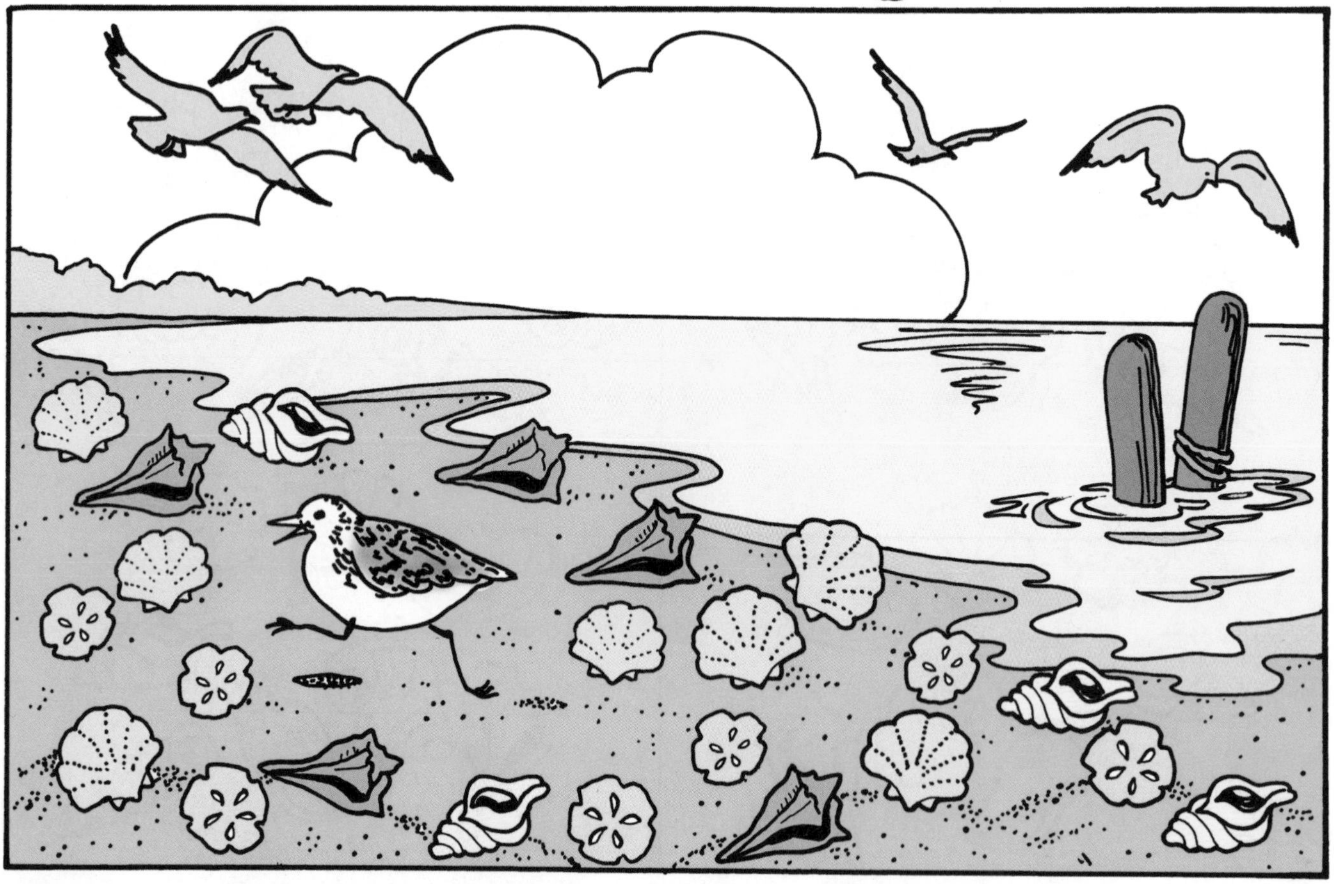

Circle the number that tells how many.

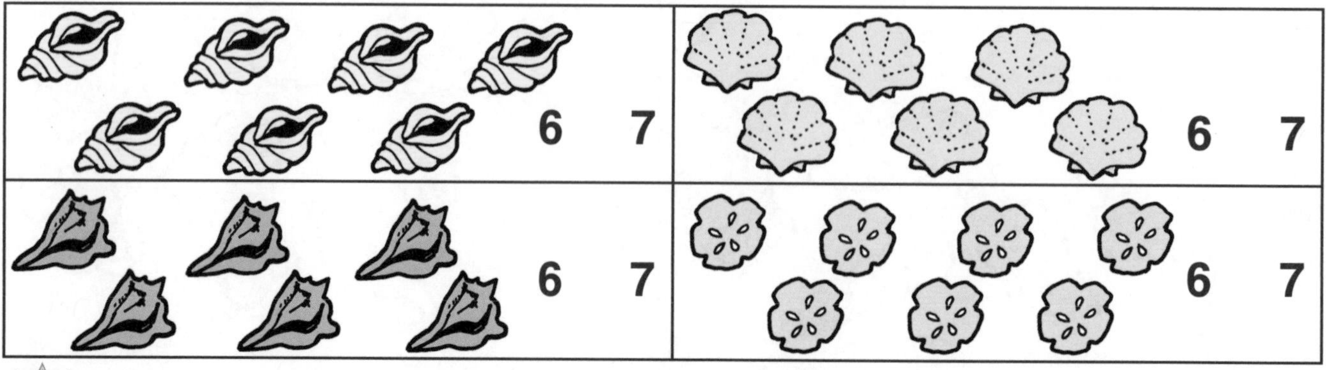

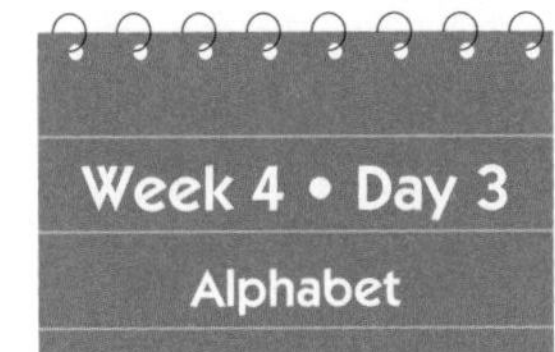

Letter E

Trace and write.

E E

e e

Circle every **E** and every **e**.

T	E	E	F	T	F	F	E
e	a	o	e	c	e	a	e

I found _______ E's and _______ e's.

Add e's and then read the words.

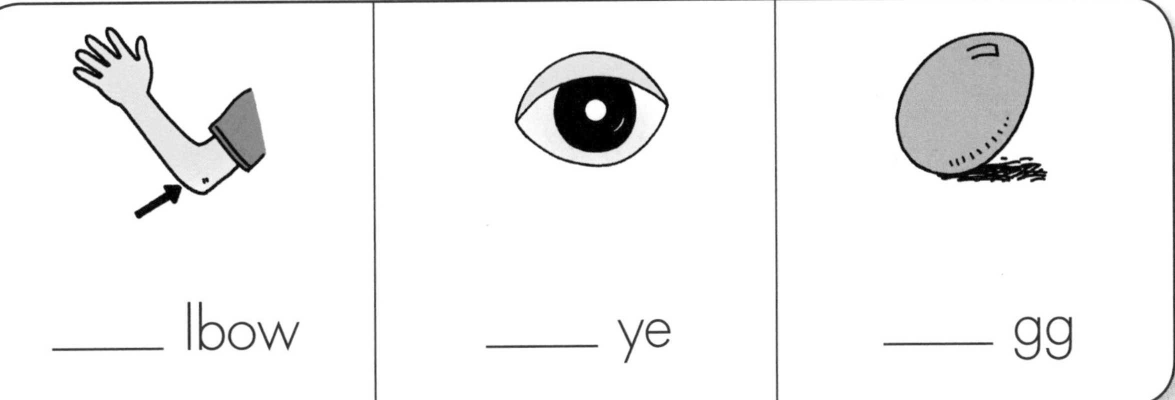

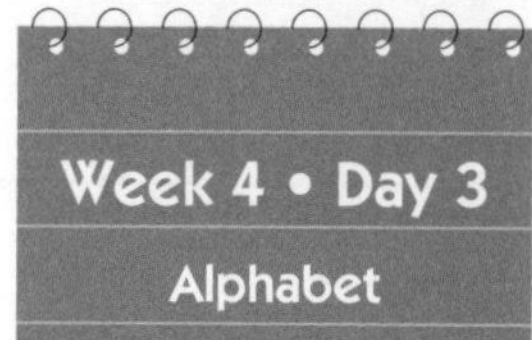

Letter F

Trace and write.

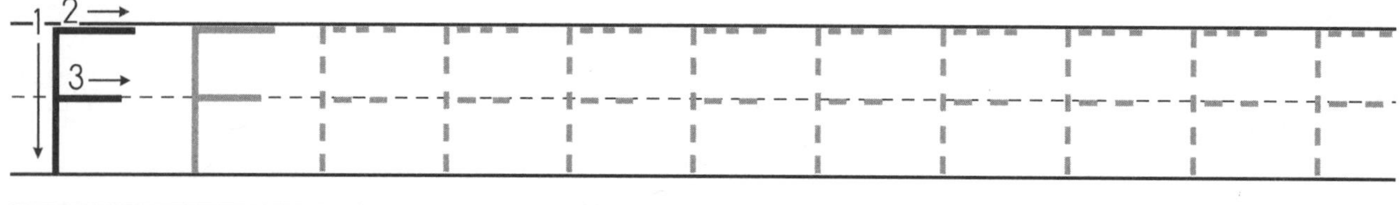

Circle every **F** and every **f**.

F E T F E E F T

f t t f l f k f

I found _______ F's and _______ f's.

Add f's and then read the words.

_____ eather

_____ ish

_____ ork

Eight Electric Eels

Trace and write.

Draw more eels to make 8.

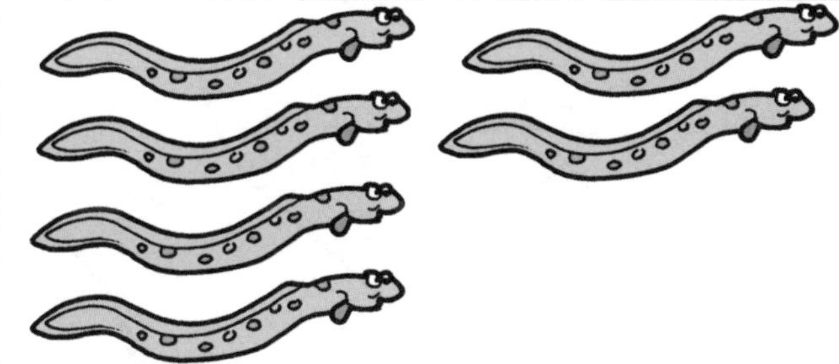

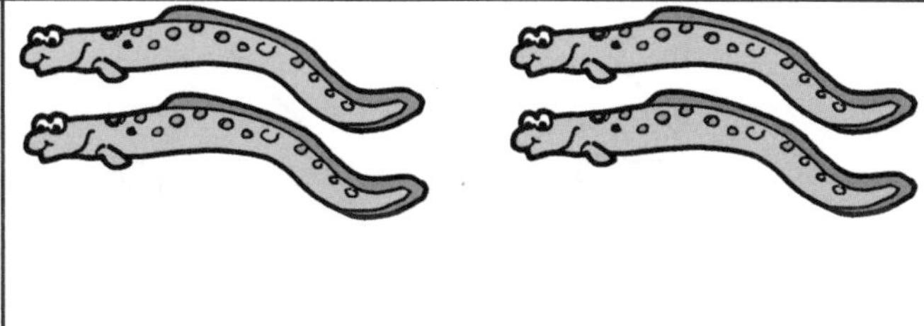

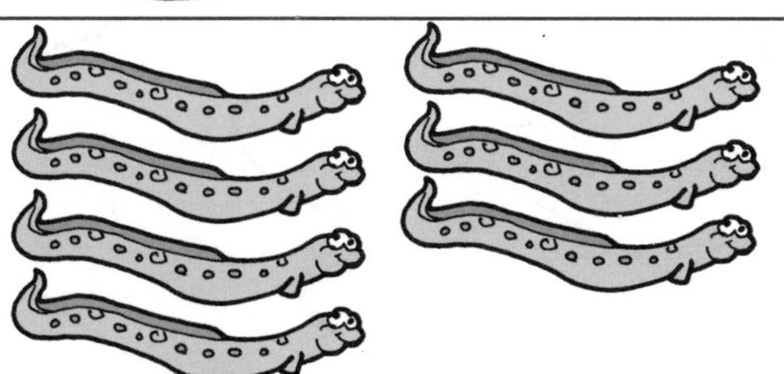

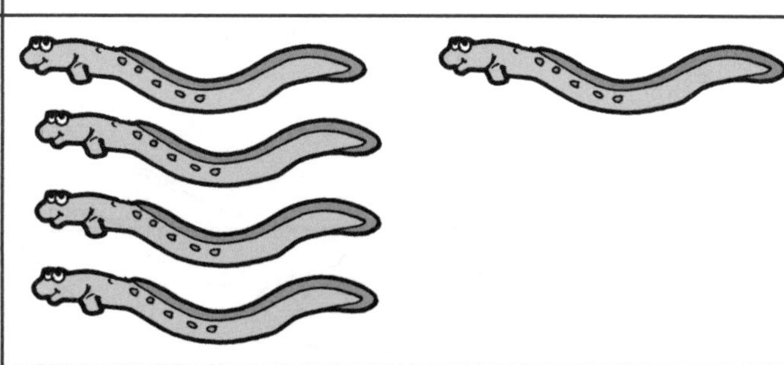

Count the eels. Color the animal with the matching number.

Eddie Eel Is Lost

Help Eddie Eel find his way back to the cave. Trace the path that goes in order from 1 to 8.

On a sheet of paper, draw a picture of 8 different sea creatures.

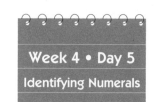

A Sea of Numbers

Color the picture using the color code.

1 

2 

3 

4 

5 

6 

7 

8 

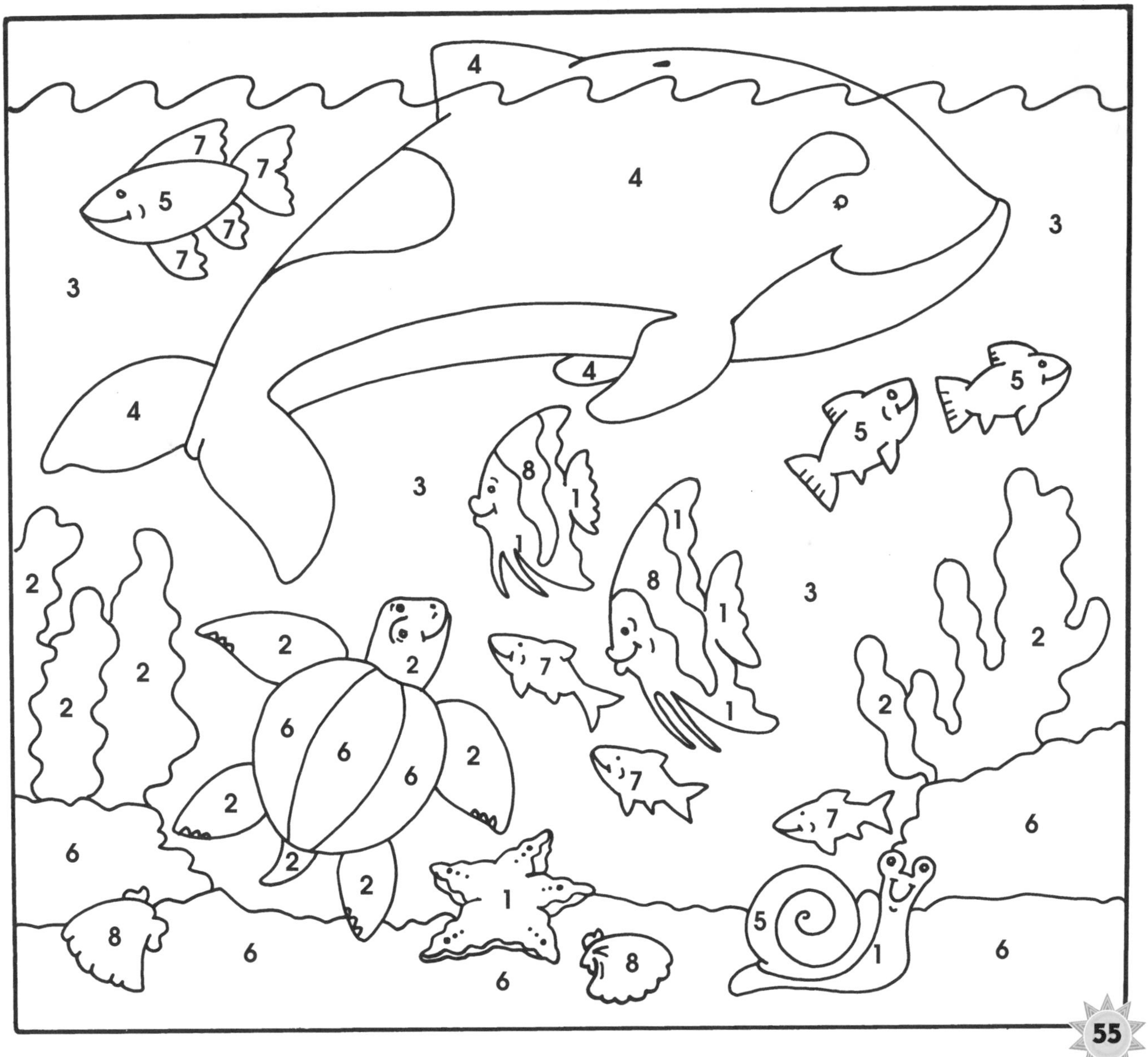

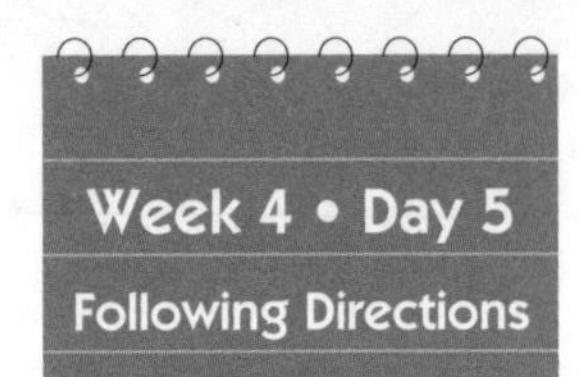

You Can Draw an Apple!

1 Draw a circle with two bumps on top.
2 Draw a rectangle for the stem.
3 Draw a pointed leaf.

______________________ 's Incentive Chart: Week 5

Name Here

This week, I plan to read __________ minutes each day.

CHART YOUR PROGRESS HERE.

Week 1	Day 1	Day 2	Day 3	Day 4	Day 5
I read for...	minutes	minutes	minutes	minutes	minutes
Put a sticker to show you completed each day's work.					

Wow! You did a great job this week!

Place sticker here.

Parent or Caregiver's Signature ______________________

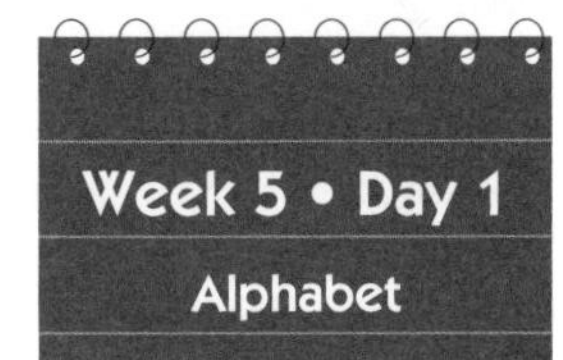

Letter G

Trace and write.

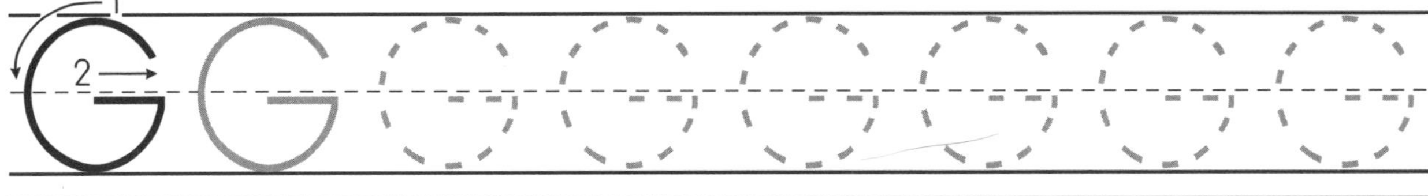

g g

Circle every **G** and every **g**.

Q G O G Q O G G

g b q g q p g g

I found ______ G's and ______ g's.

Add g's and then read the words.

_____ ame

_____ uitar

_____ ate

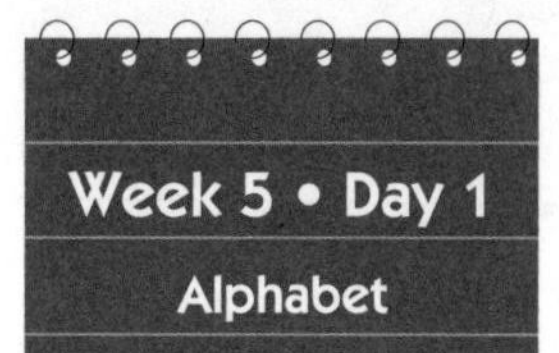

Letter H

Trace and write.

H H

h h

Circle every **H** and every **h**.

T H H T L H L H

b h l p h l h b

I found ______ H's and ______ h's.

Add h's and then read the words.

_____ air	_____ at	_____ ouse

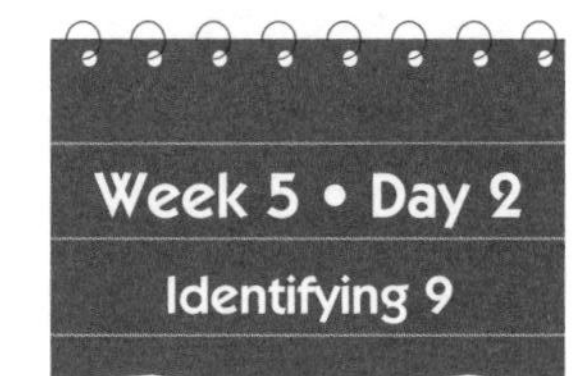

Nine Nice Nectarines

Trace and write.

9

Color each basket that has 9 pieces of fruit.

Going to the Market

FRESH FRUIT

Count the fruits. Write how many.
Color each fruit that has 9.

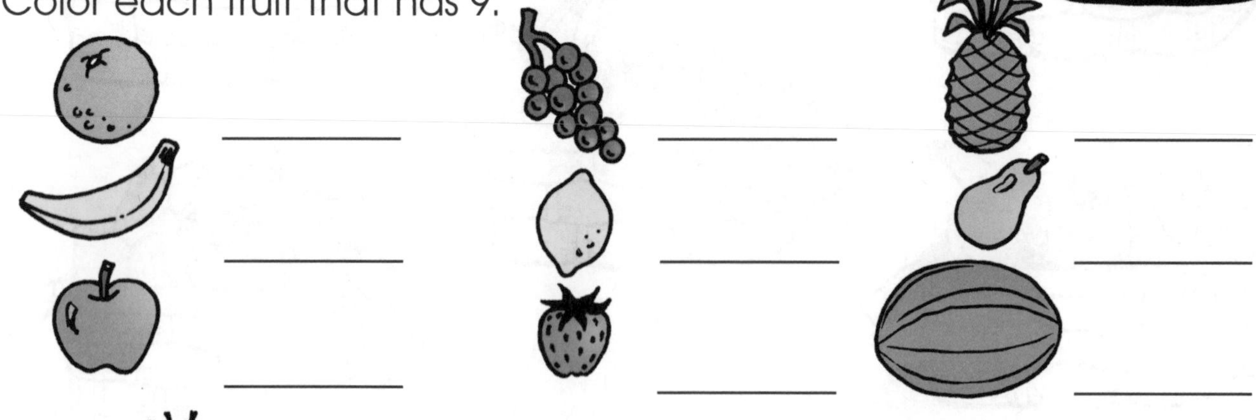

On a sheet of paper, draw 9 pieces of your favorite fruit.

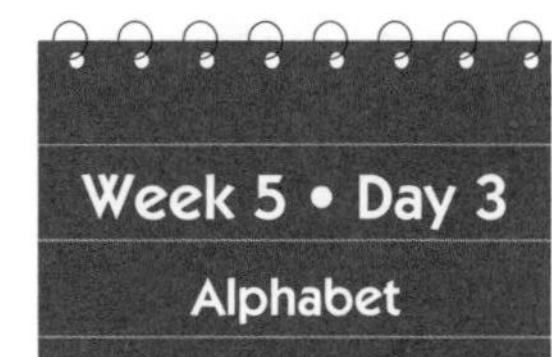

Letter I

Trace and write.

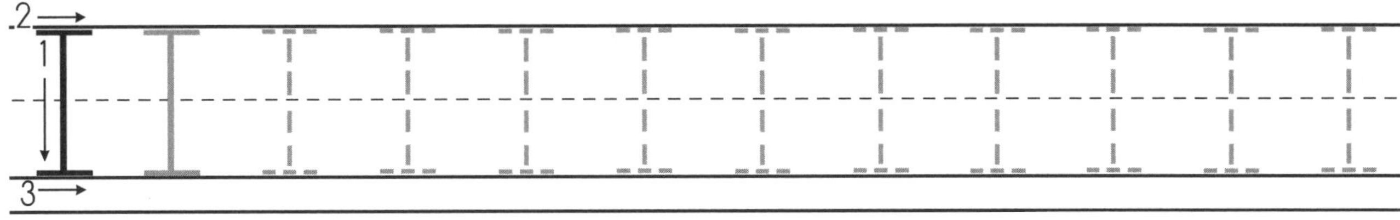

Circle every **I** and every **i**.

L	I	F	L	I	J	I	I
i	l	f	i	i	l	f	i

I found _____ I's and _____ i's.

Add i's and then read the words.

	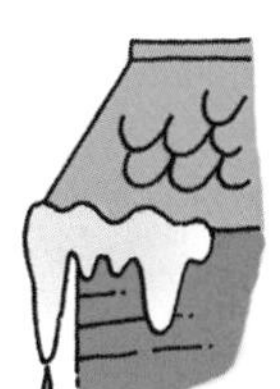	
_____ ce cream	_____ cicle	_____ ron

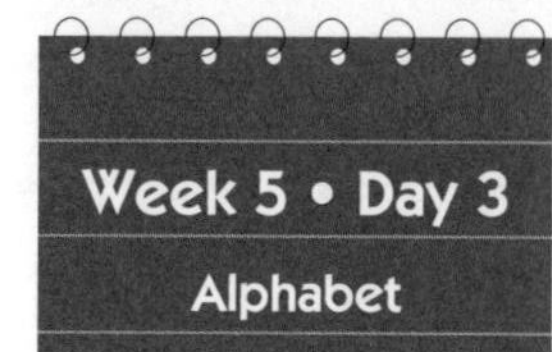

Letter J

Trace and write.

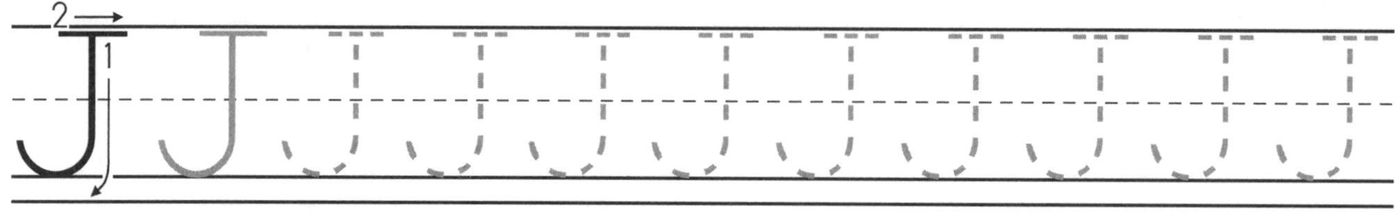

J j j j j j j j j j j j j j

Circle every **J** and every **j**.

I T J J T J K J

j g i g j p j q

I found ______ J's and ______ j's.

Add j's and then read the words.

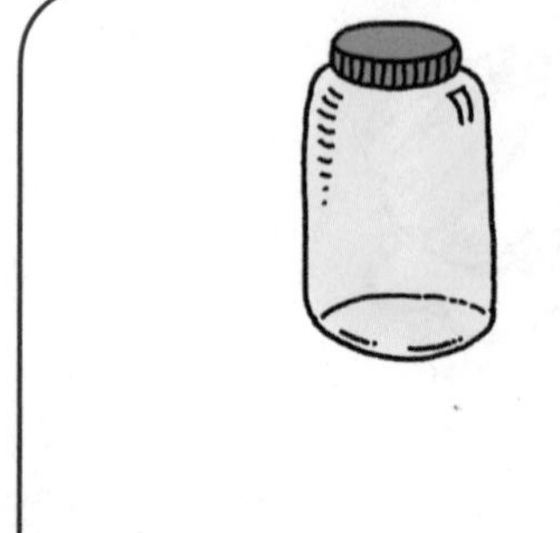		
____ ar	____ ump	____ eans

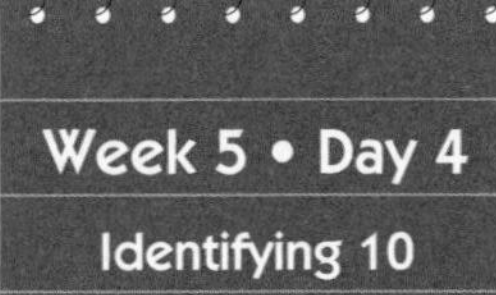

Ten Railroad Ties

Trace and write.

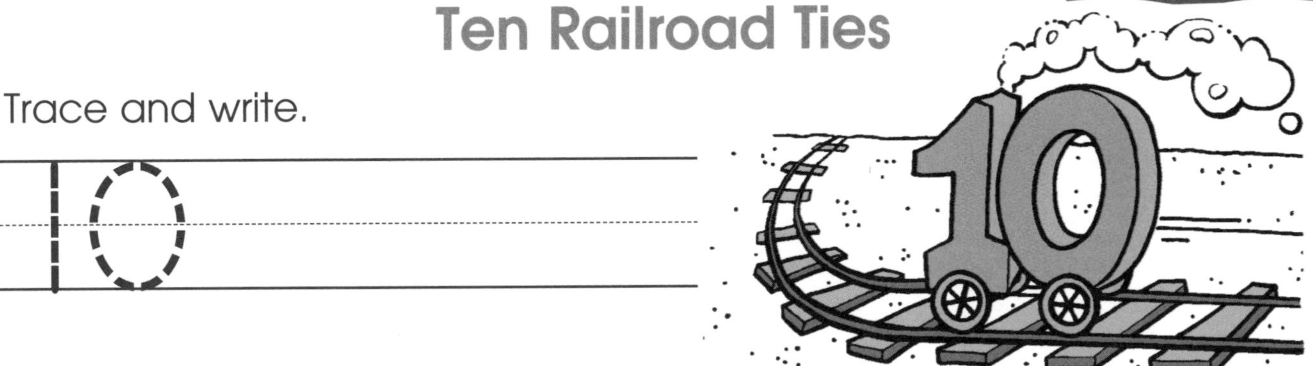

Help Tina Train find the right track. Count each railroad tie.

Color the track with 10 railroad ties red.

All Aboard

Color each train car with 8 barrels red.
Color each train car with 9 barrels blue.
Color each train car with 10 barrels green.

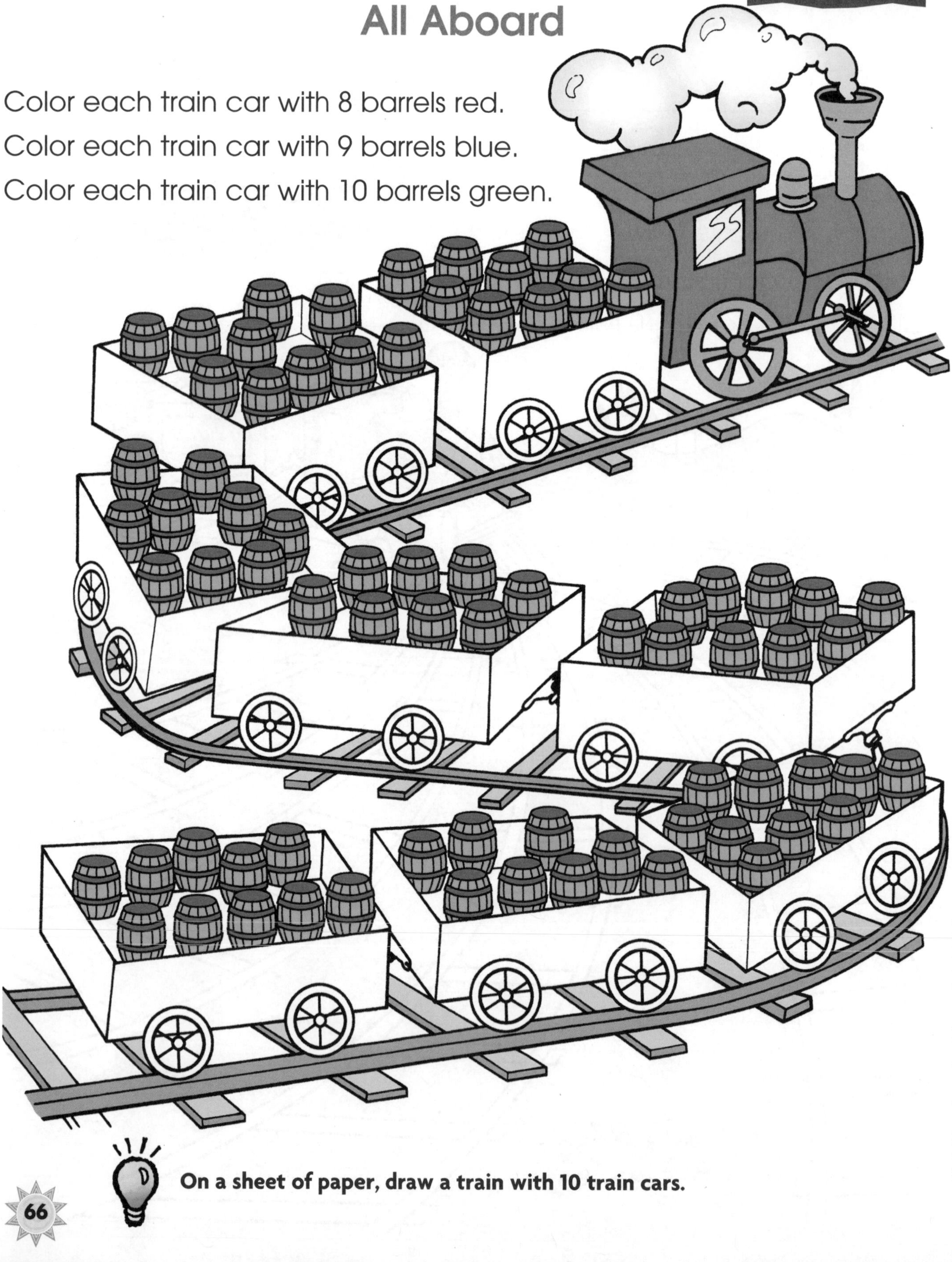

On a sheet of paper, draw a train with 10 train cars.

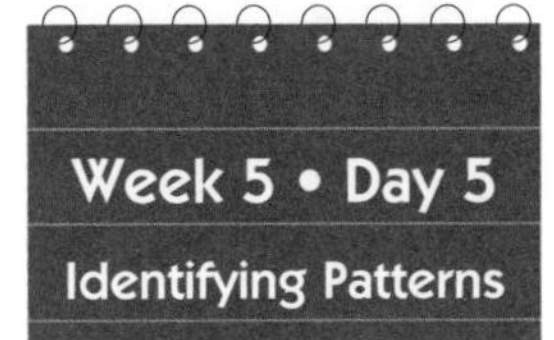

What Comes Next?

Circle the shape that comes next.

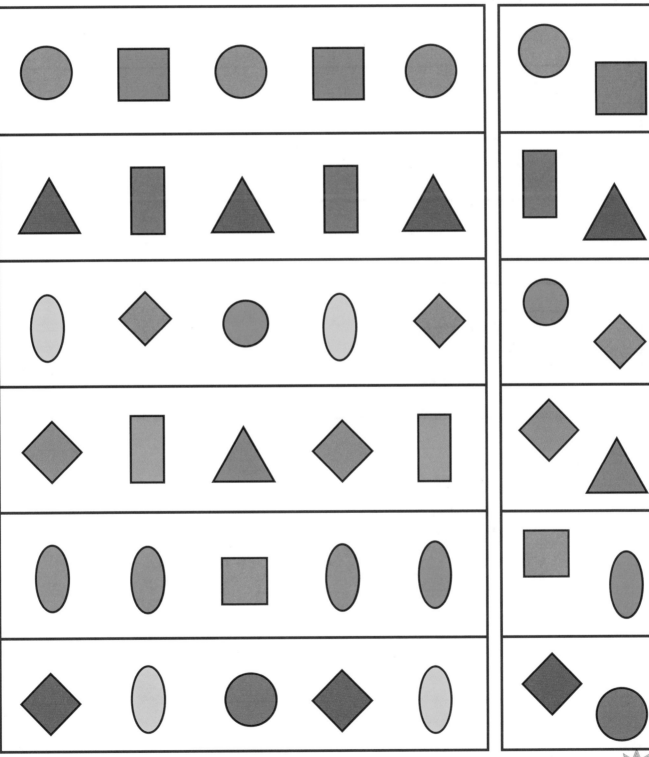

Decorate a Headband

Draw the shapes that finish the patterns. Then color and cut out. Attach lengths of yarn to both ends of the patterns to form headbands.

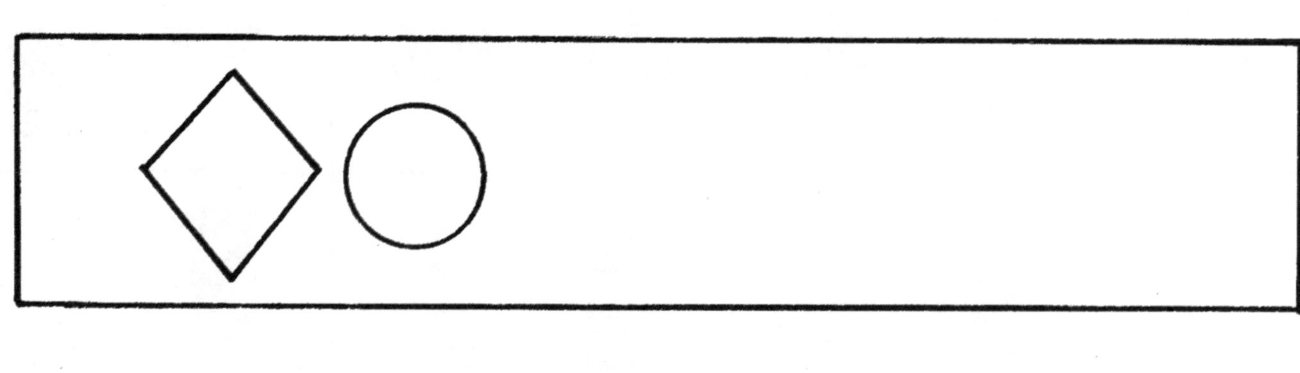

______________________ 's Incentive Chart: Week 6

Name Here

This week, I plan to read __________ minutes each day.

CHART YOUR PROGRESS HERE.

Week 1	Day 1	Day 2	Day 3	Day 4	Day 5
I read for...	minutes	minutes	minutes	minutes	minutes
Put a sticker to show you completed each day's work.					

Congratulations!

Wow! You did a great job this week!

Parent or Caregiver's Signature ______________________________

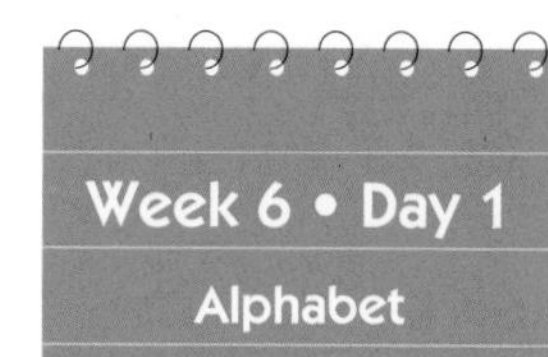

Letter K

Trace and write.

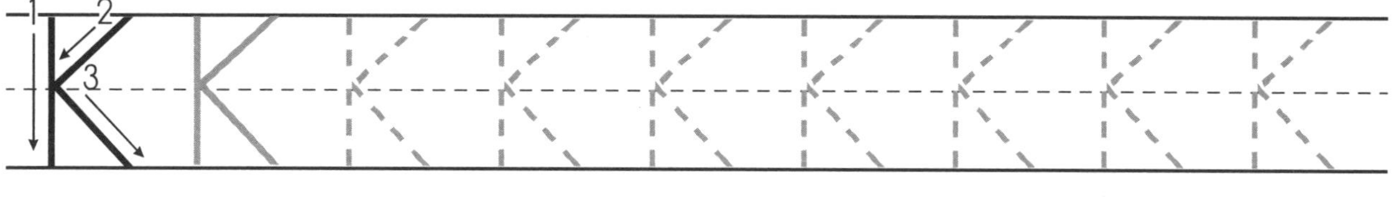

Circle every **K** and every **k**.

S	K	X	S	K	X	S	X
k	t	f	f	k	x	k	k

I found ______ K's and ______ k's.

Add k's and then read the words.

	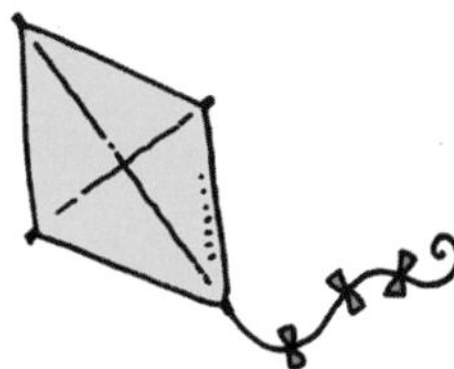	
_____ ing	_____ ite	_____ angaroo

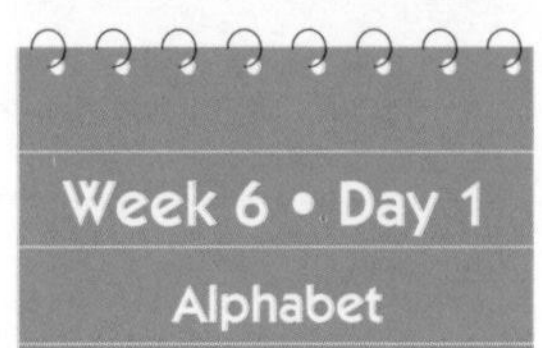

Letter L

Trace and write.

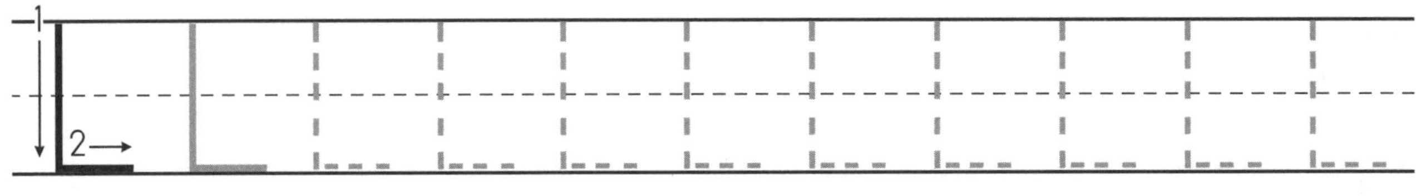

Circle every **L** and every **l**.

L H I L L I L H

l i l l i l t h

I found ______ L's and ______ l's.

Add l's and then read the words.

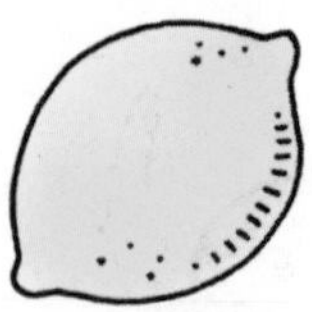		
_____ emon	_____ eaf	_____ ion

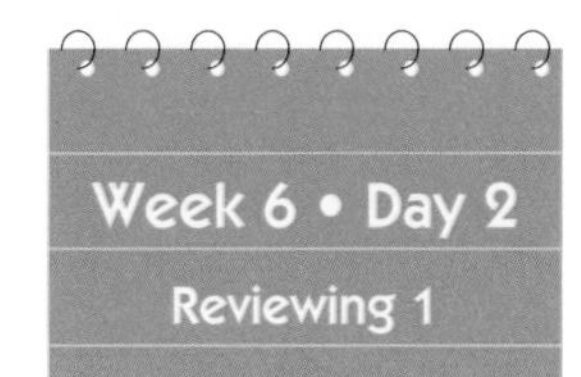

Number Practice: 1

Trace the number.

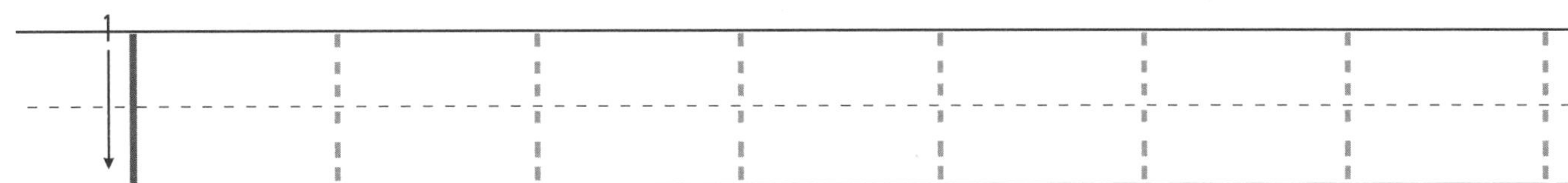

Write the number.

Trace the word.

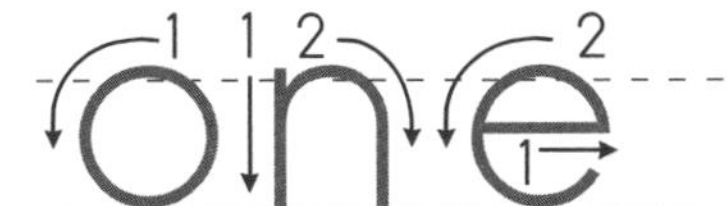

Write the word.

Number Hunt

Circle every number 1.

6 3 1 8 9 22 8 30 0 1 27

20 2 4 6 1 5 9 1 5 26 3

5 22 6 7 8 1 27 0 3 4 1

1 23 8 1 29 0 4 7 9 3 1

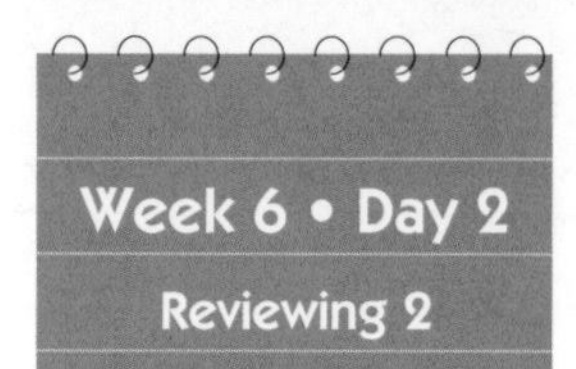

Number Practice: 2

Trace the number.

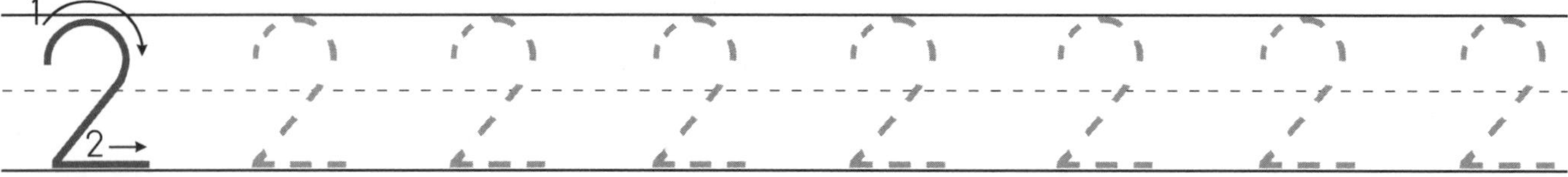

Write the number.

Trace the word.

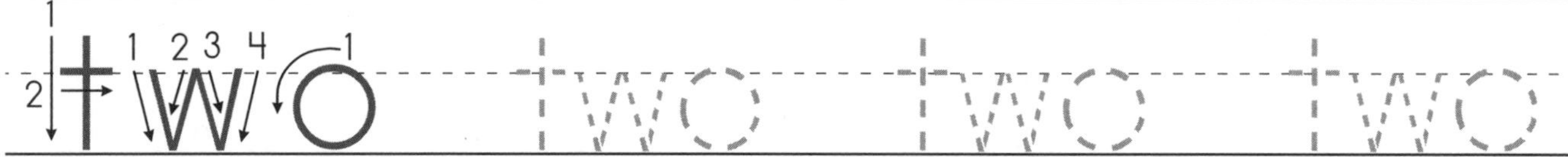

Write the word.

Number Hunt

Circle every number 2.

13	0	4	6	19	2	30	2	0	17
2	9	3	14	0	2	11	5	6	15
17	3	2	6	16	8	10	7	9	2
19	2	18	9	5	4	2	0	1	16

Letter M

Trace and write.

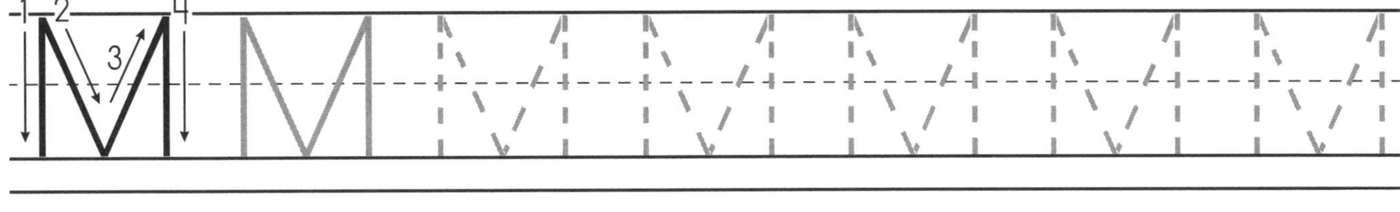

Circle every **M** and every **m**.

M N V N N M W M

m n v w m m n m

I found ______ M's and ______ m's.

Add m's and then read the words.

	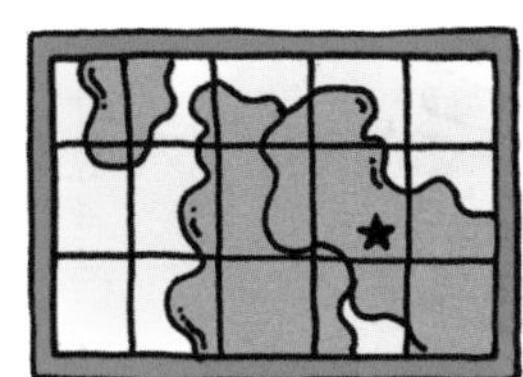	
_____ ouse	_____ ap	_____ onkey

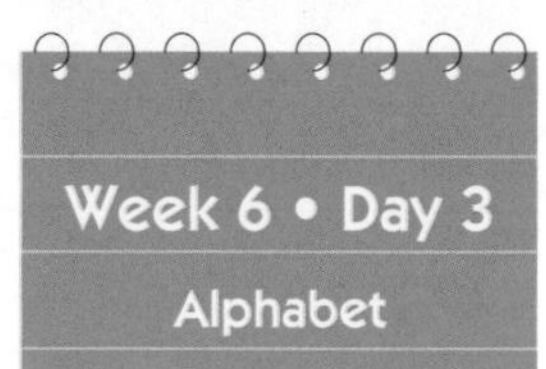

Letter N

Trace and write.

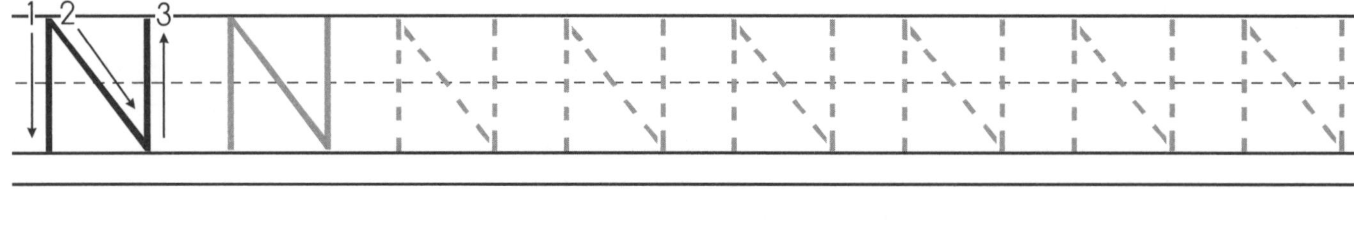

1 2 3 N N

1 2 n n

Circle every **N** and every **n**.

N M N V N W N N

n m n u m m n u

I found _______ N's and _______ n's.

Add n's and then read the words.

_____ est	_____ ewspaper	_____ ut

Size It Up

Draw a ◇ around the picture that is **short**.

Draw a ◇ around the picture that is **long**.

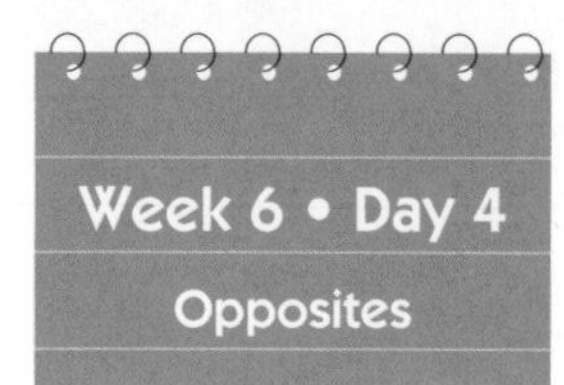

Transportation Station

Draw a ▭ around the picture that is **big**.

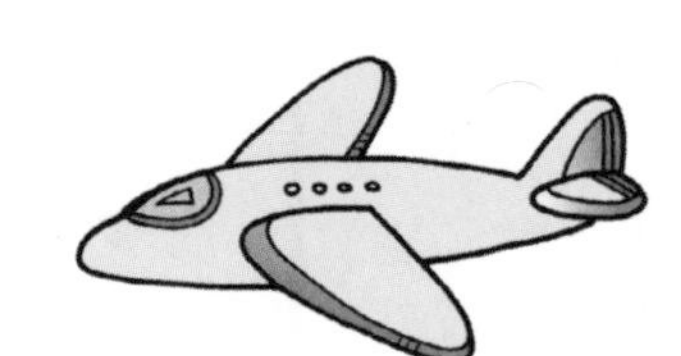

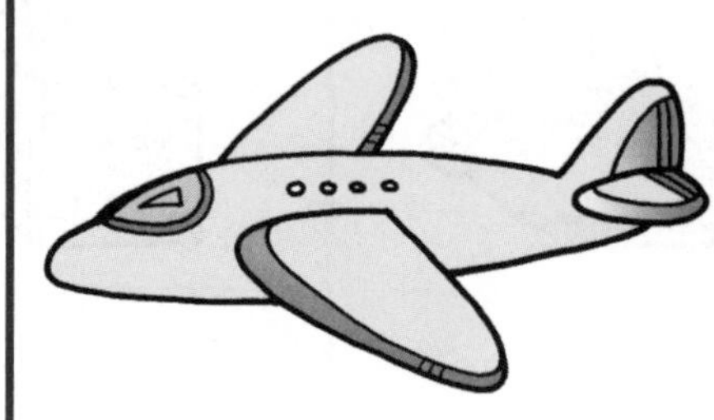

Draw a ▭ around the picture that is **small**.

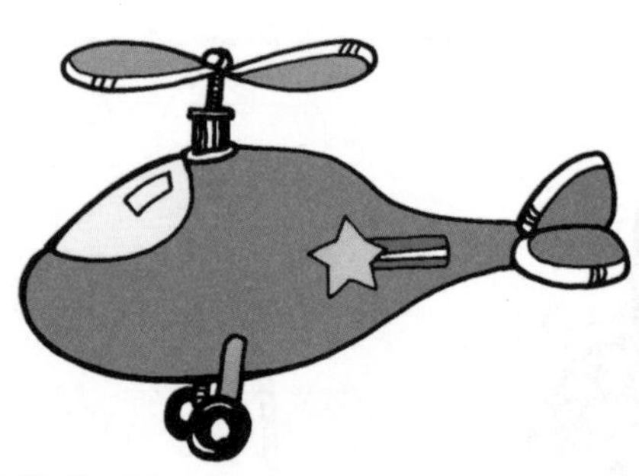

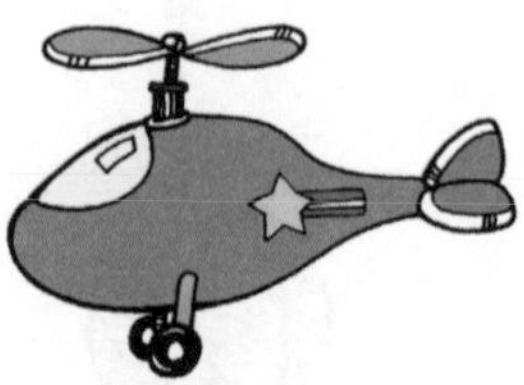

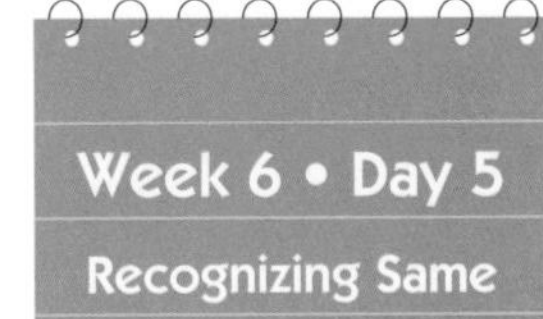

A Perfect Match

 and  are the **same**.

Connect the cars that are the same.

Name one way you and a friend are the same.

You Can Draw a Balloon!

_______________ 's Incentive Chart: Week 7

Name Here

This week, I plan to read __________ minutes each day.

CHART YOUR PROGRESS HERE.

Week 1	Day 1	Day 2	Day 3	Day 4	Day 5
I read for...	minutes	minutes	minutes	minutes	minutes
Put a sticker to show you completed each day's work.					

Congratulations!

Wow! You did a great job this week!

#1

Place sticker here.

Parent or Caregiver's Signature ______________________________

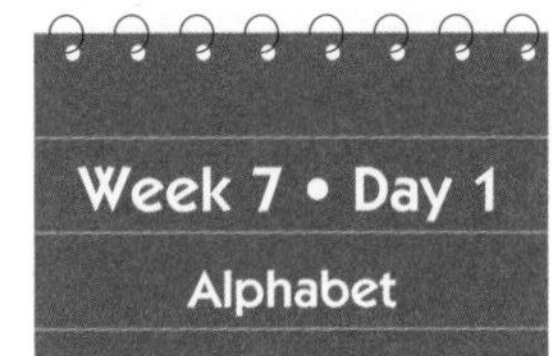

Letter O

Trace and write.

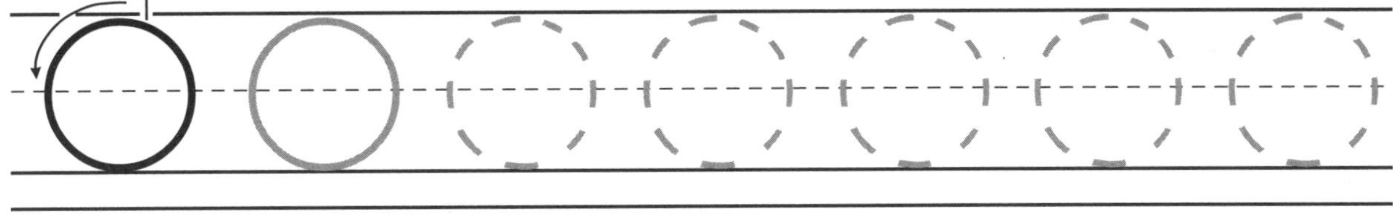

Circle every **O** and every **o**.

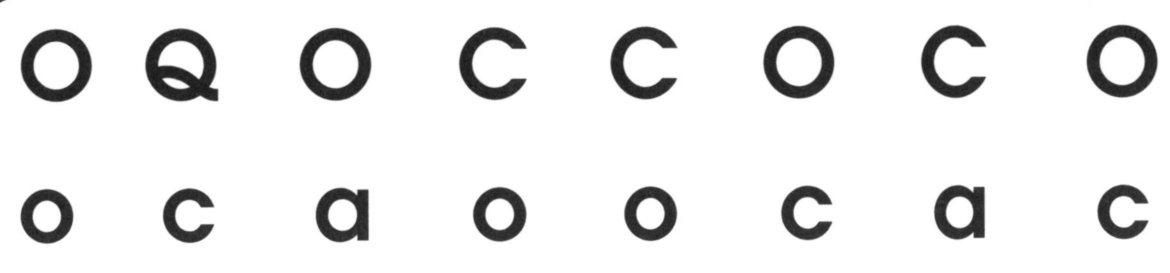

I found ______ O's and ______ o's.

Add o's and then read the words.

____ wl	____ ctopus	____ ven

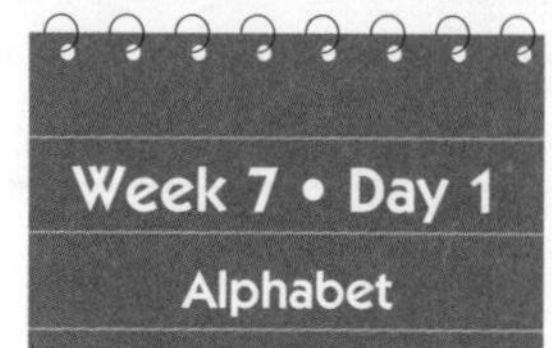

Letter P

Trace and write.

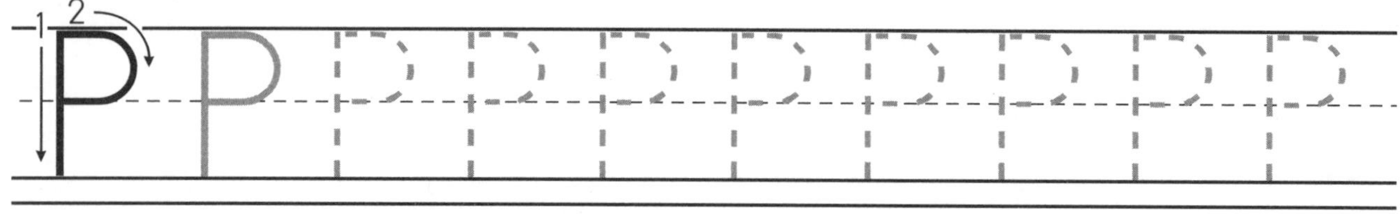

Circle every **P** and every **p**.

P R P B R B P R

p q b d p b q p

I found ______ P's and ______ p's.

Add p's and then read the words.

_____ ail	_____ encil	_____ an

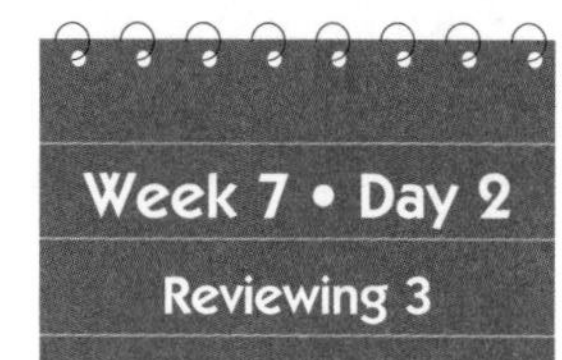

Number Practice: 3

Trace the number.

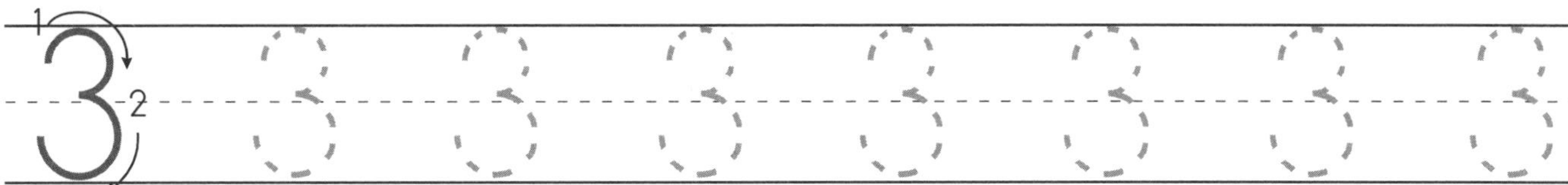

Write the number.

Trace the word.

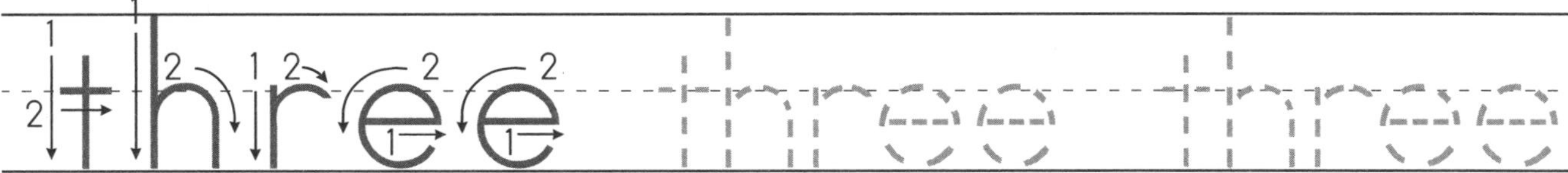

Write the word.

Number Hunt

Circle every number 3.

0	3	1	8	13	9	25	2	4	26
21	5	7	12	3	25	3	9	8	1
8	16	24	3	0	5	4	3	20	0
3	0	29	1	3	7	19	8	10	14

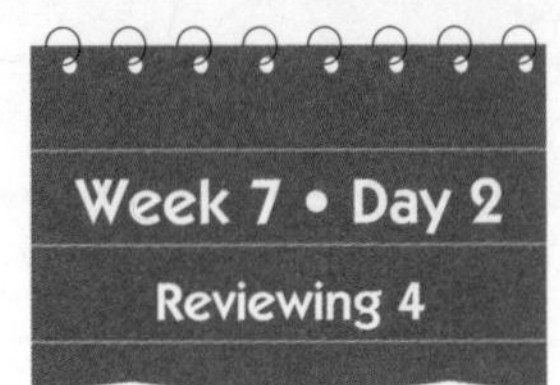

Number Practice: 4

Trace the number.

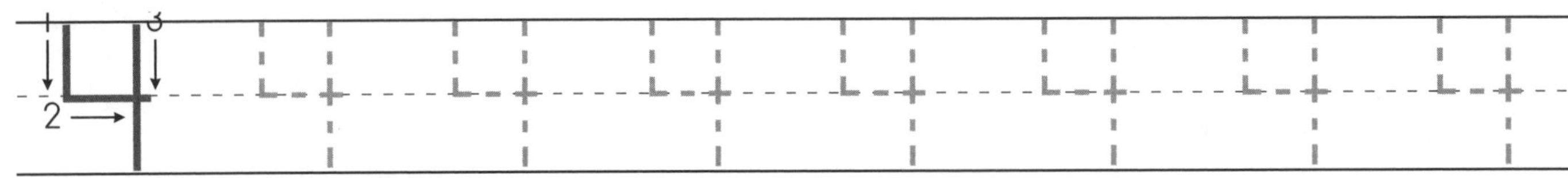

Write the number.

Trace the word.

Write the word.

Number Hunt

Circle every number 4.

30	16	25	4	6	3	18	0	9	27	29
1	10	20	1	5	10	4	6	9	6	22
5	18	21	4	13	5	28	4	9	0	11
7	26	4	6	3	7	22	7	8	9	29

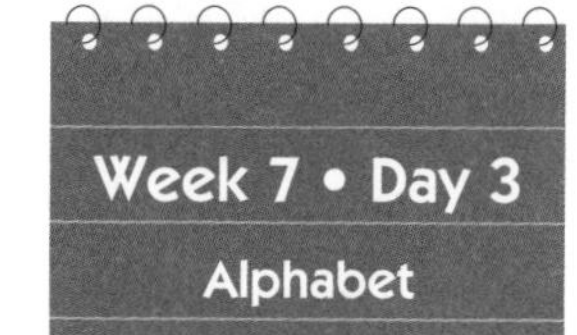

Letter Q

Trace and write.

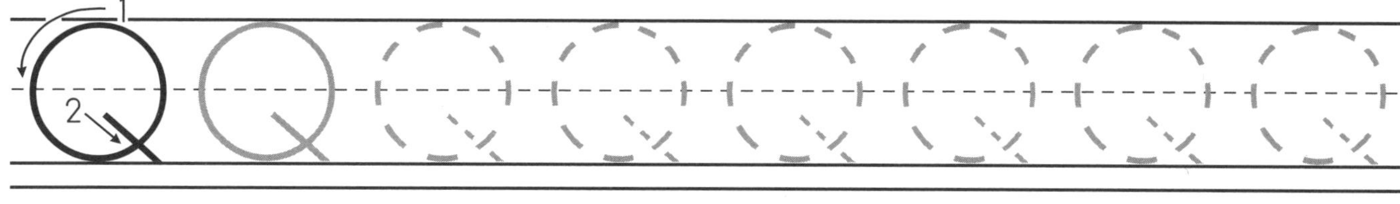

Q Q Q Q Q Q Q Q

q q q q q q q q q q q q

Circle every **Q** and every **q**.

Q C O C Q O Q C

q g p g b d q g

I found ______ Q's and ______ q's.

Add q's and then read the words.

_____ ueen	_____ uilt	_____ uiet

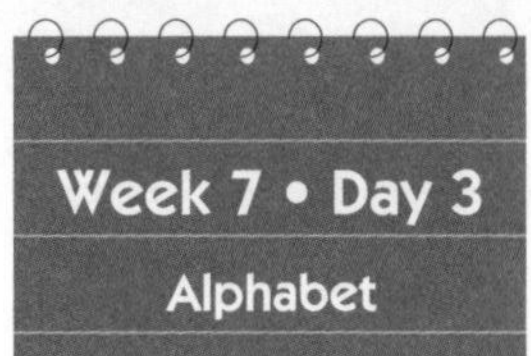

Letter R

Trace and write.

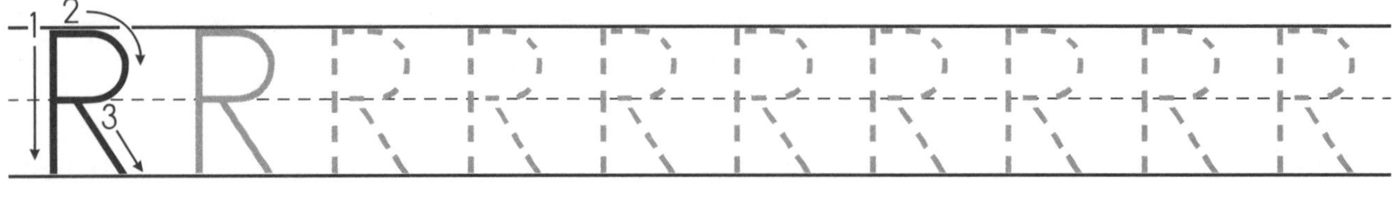

r r

Circle every **R** and every **r**.

R B P R R R B P

r t n i r r n t

I found ______ R's and ______ r's.

Add r's and then read the words.

____ abbit	____ ope	____ ocket

Searching for Opposites

An elephant is big. A mouse is little.
Big and little are **opposites**.
Circle the picture that shows the opposite.

happy	sad
up	down
boy	girl
fast	slow

Name something you can do fast. Name something you can do slow.

Searching for More Opposites

Circle the picture that shows the **opposite**.

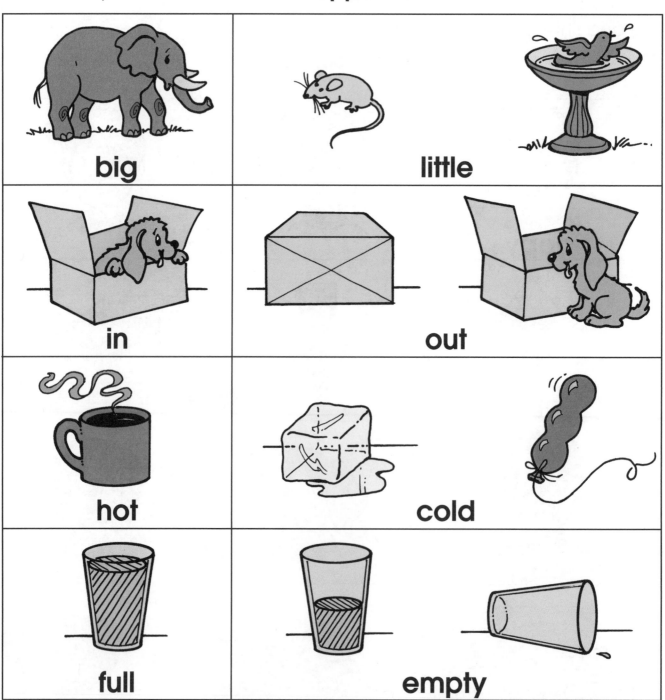

 big	  little
 in	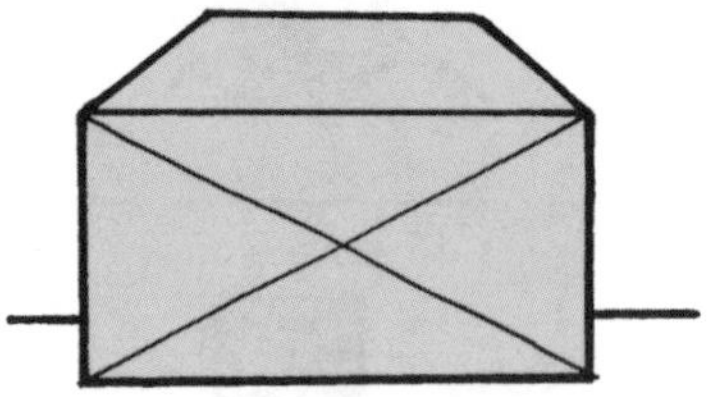  out
 hot	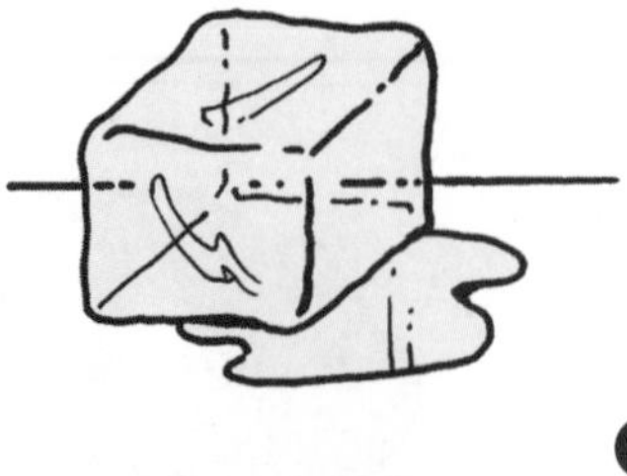  cold
 full	 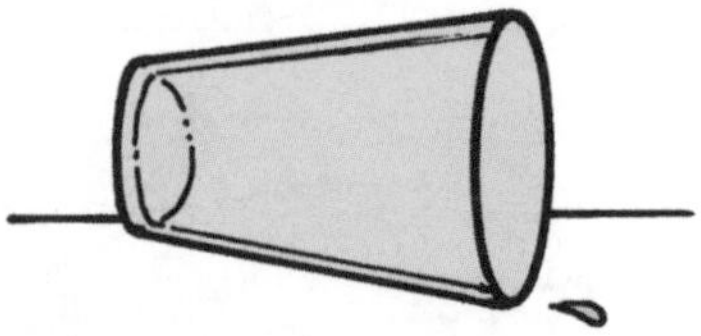 empty

On a sheet of paper, draw a picture of a something that might be larger than an elephant.

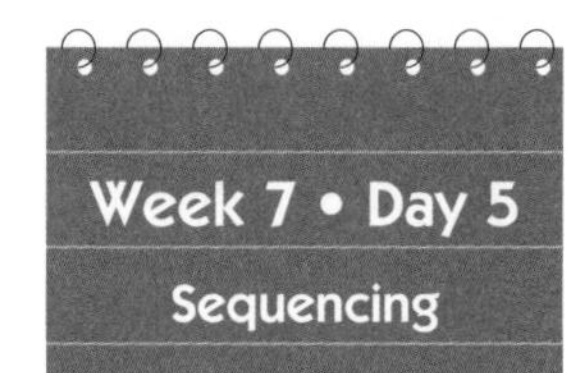

Everything in Order

The **sequence** is the order in which things happen.

Write 1 under the picture that happens first.
Write 2 under the picture that happens second.

______ ______

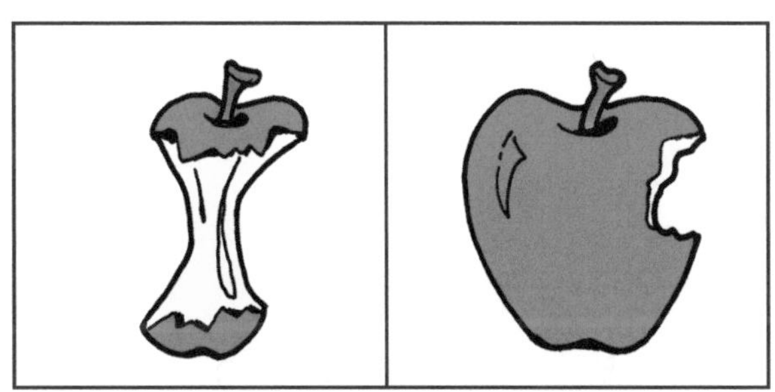

______ ______

______ ______

______ ______

______ ______

______ ______

What do you do first when you wake up?

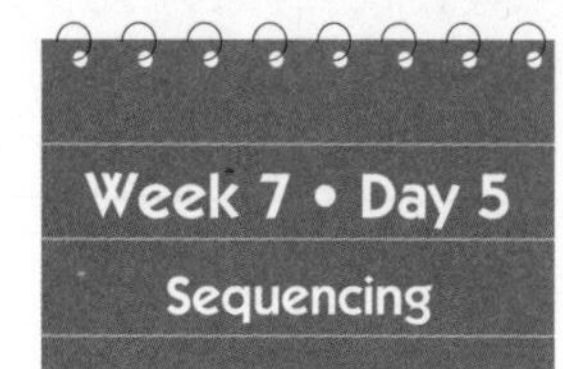

Perfect Order

Write 1 by what happened first.

Write 2 by what happened second.

Write 3 by what happened third.

______________________ 's Incentive Chart: Week 8

Name Here

This week, I plan to read __________ minutes each day.

CHART YOUR PROGRESS HERE.

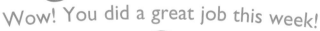

Week 1	Day 1	Day 2	Day 3	Day 4	Day 5
I read for...	minutes	minutes	minutes	minutes	minutes
Put a sticker to show you completed each day's work.					

Congratulations!

Wow! You did a great job this week!

Place sticker here.

Parent or Caregiver's Signature ______________________

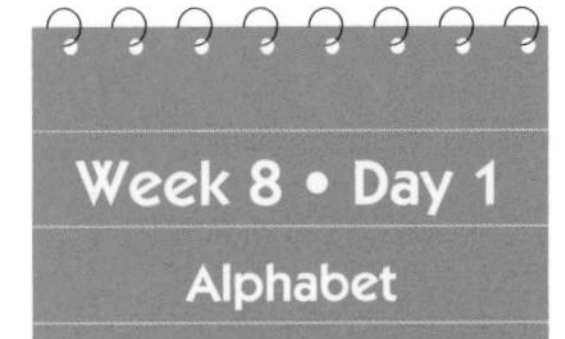

Letter S

Trace and write.

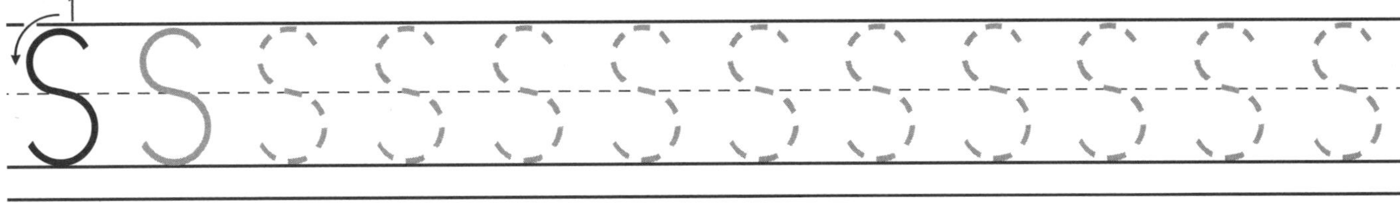

S S

Circle every **S** and every **s**.

S R S D S R S S

s c e s s e c s

I found _______ S's and _______ s's.

Add s's and then read the words.

	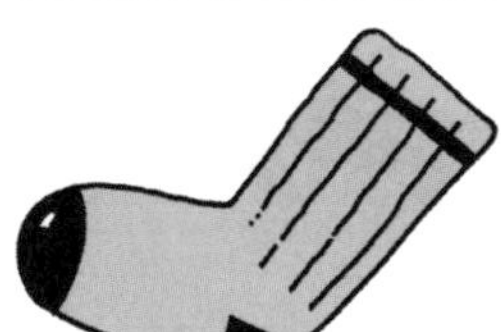	
_____ andwich	_____ ock	_____ oap

Letter T

Trace and write.

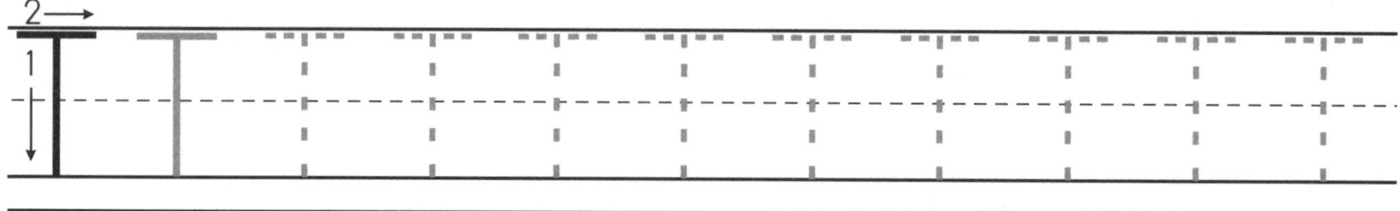

Circle every **T** and every **t**.

T	I	F	L	T	F	T	L
t	f	l	t	i	t	l	t

I found ______ T's and ______ t's.

Add t's and then read the words.

_____ ent	_____ oothbrush	_____ ub

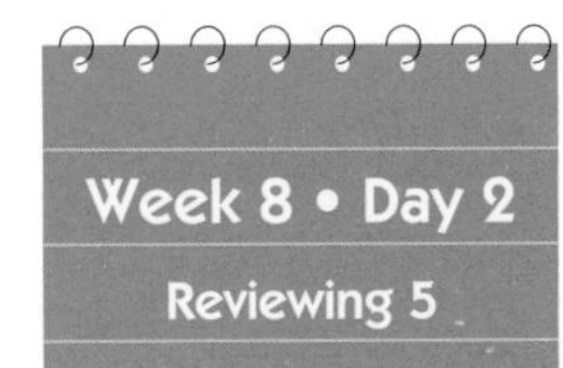

Number Practice: 5

Trace the number.

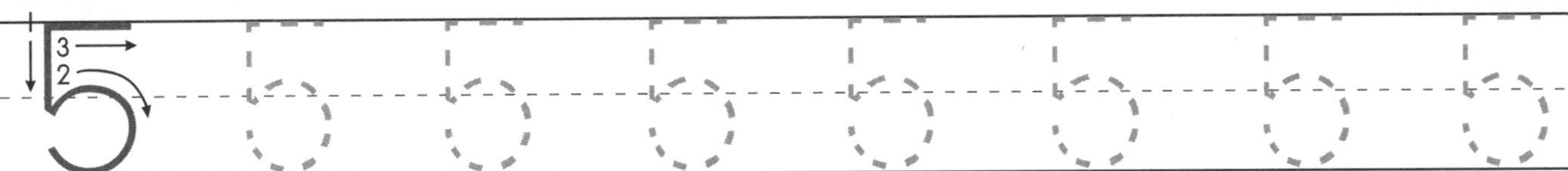

Write the number.

Trace the word.

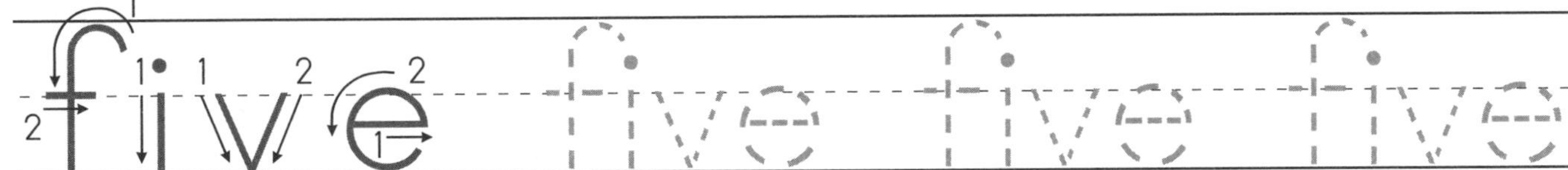

Write the word.

Number Hunt

Circle every number 5.

2	5	3	0	1	4	5	8	9	6	10
6	4	18	5	2	1	7	5	0	9	5
7	3	8	1	9	5	16	7	0	1	4
11	4	5	9	21	3	9	2	1	10	8

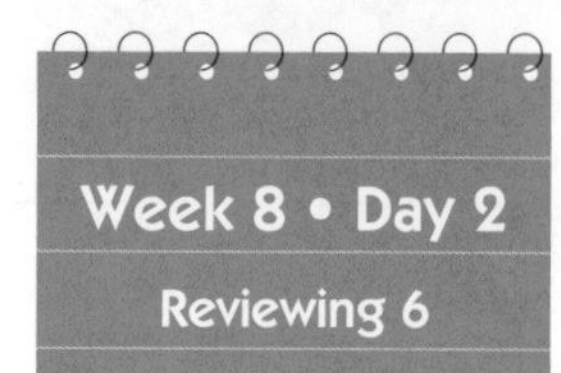

Number Practice: 6

Trace the number.

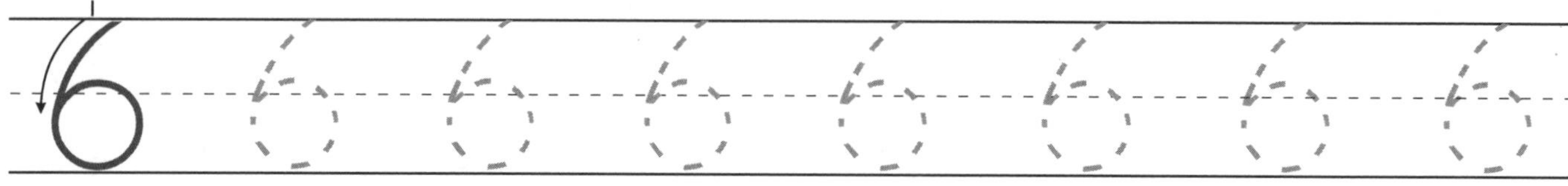

Write the number.

Trace the word.

Write the word.

Number Hunt

Circle every number 6.

0	2	1	8	13	9	25	2	6	20	5
28	6	7	12	9	25	3	6	8	1	9
6	17	2	6	3	0	5	6	3	20	0
0	29	1	3	7	19	8	10	1	6	8

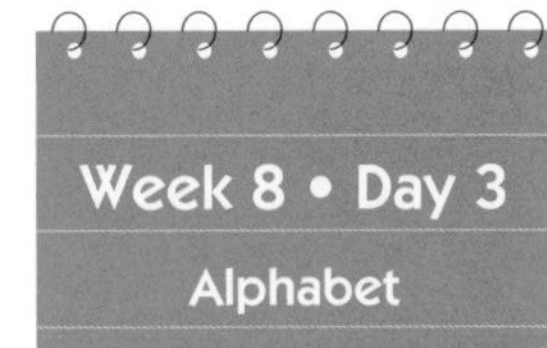

Letter U

Trace and write.

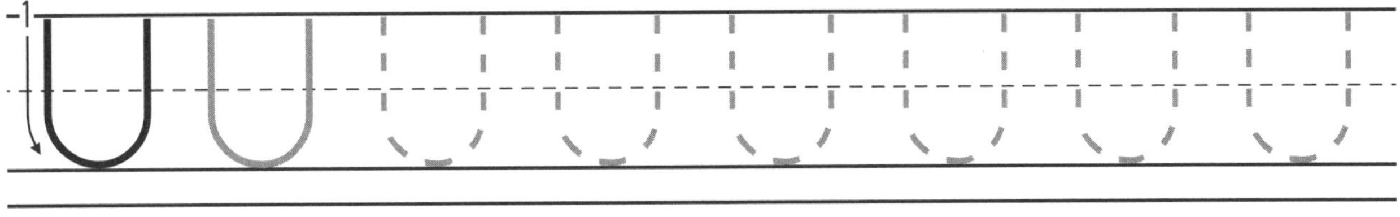

Circle every **U** and every **u**.

C U V C O V U O

u c n u y u u y

I found ______ U's and ______ u's.

Add u's and then read the words.

____ mbrella	____ nicorn	____ p

Letter V

Trace and write.

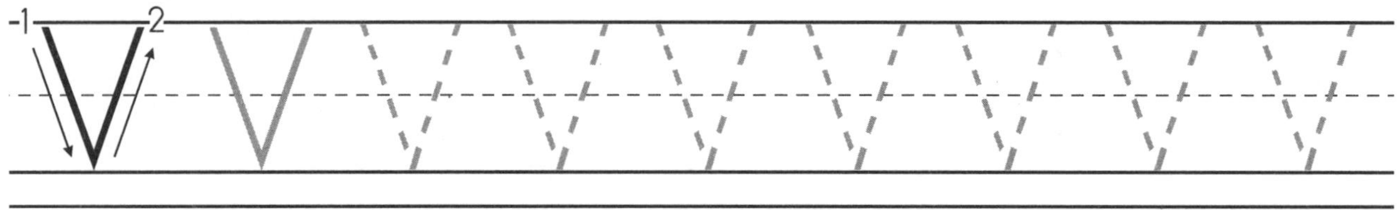

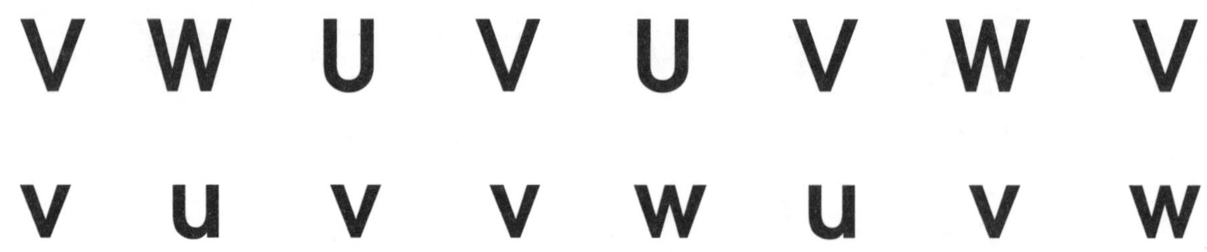

Circle every **V** and every **v**.

V W U V U V W V

v u v v w u v w

I found ______ V's and ______ v's.

Add v's and then read the words.

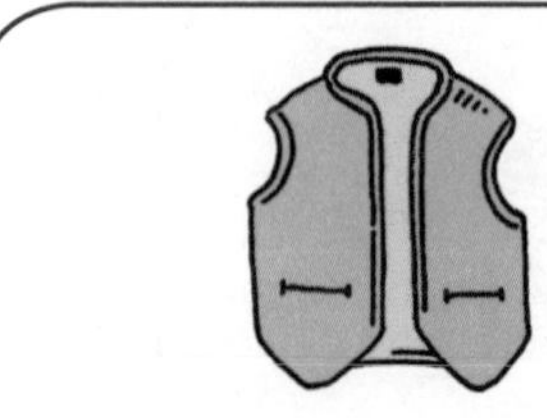	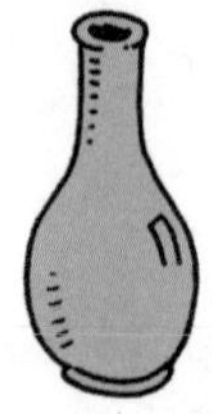	
____ est	____ ase	____ an

Picking Flowers

Circle what comes next.

Side by Side

Draw a line to match the pictures that go together.

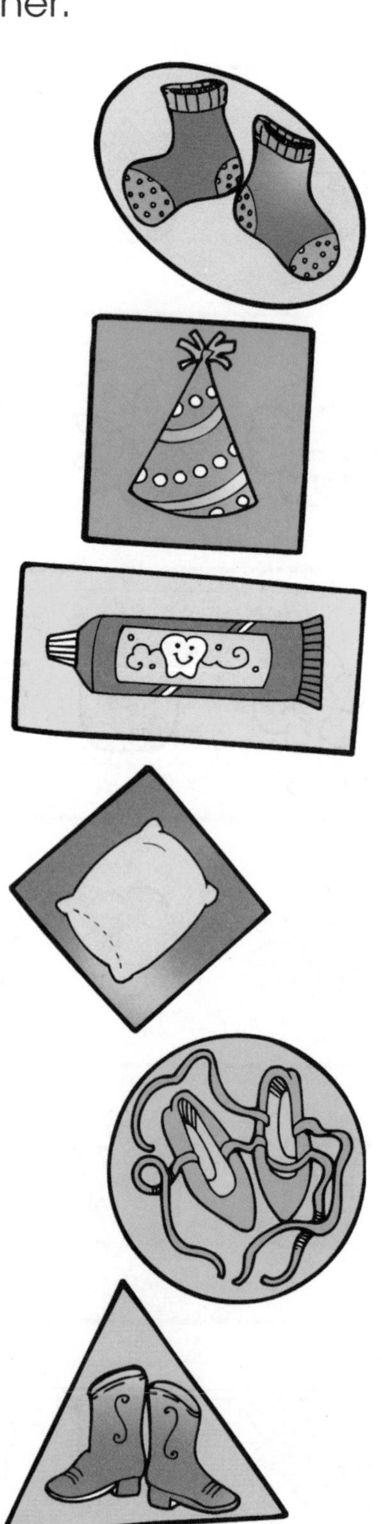

Out of Place

Put an **X** on the picture that does not belong.

You Can Draw a Kite!

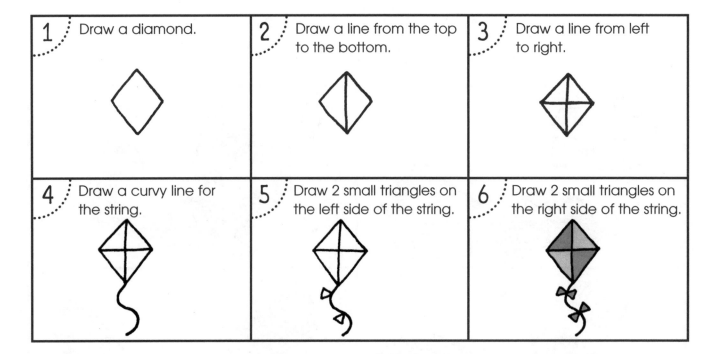

1 Draw a diamond.	2 Draw a line from the top to the bottom.	3 Draw a line from left to right.
4 Draw a curvy line for the string.	5 Draw 2 small triangles on the left side of the string.	6 Draw 2 small triangles on the right side of the string.

_______________ 's Incentive Chart: Week 9

Name Here

This week, I plan to read __________ minutes each day.

CHART YOUR PROGRESS HERE.

Week 1	Day 1	Day 2	Day 3	Day 4	Day 5
I read for...	minutes	minutes	minutes	minutes	minutes
Put a sticker to show you completed each day's work.					

Congratulations!

Wow! You did a great job this week!

Place sticker here.

Parent or Caregiver's Signature ______________________________

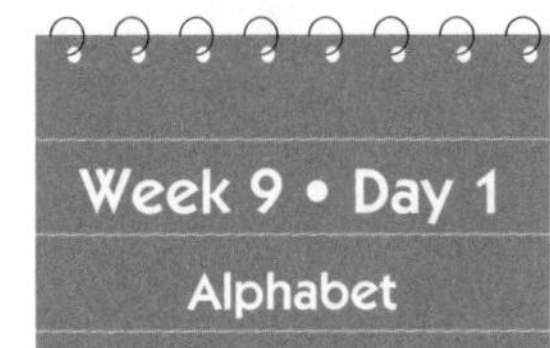

Letter W

Trace and write.

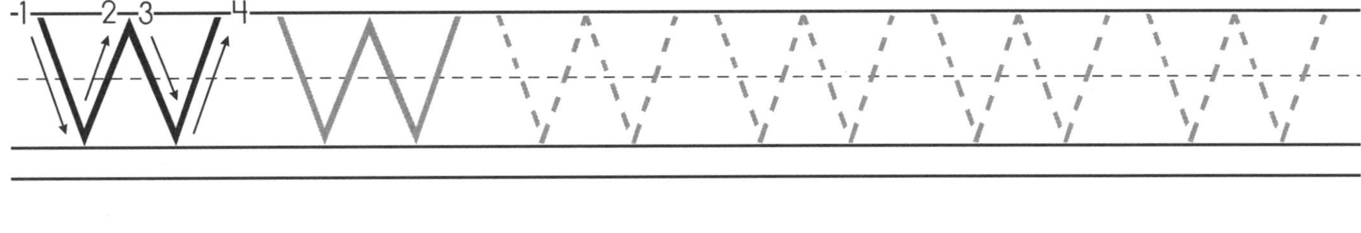

W W

Circle every **W** and every **w**.

W V M V U W V M

w v u m w w m w

I found ______ W's and ______ w's.

Add w's and then read the words.

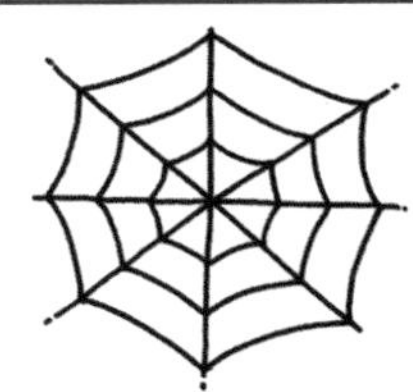		
_____ eb	_____ orm	_____ indow

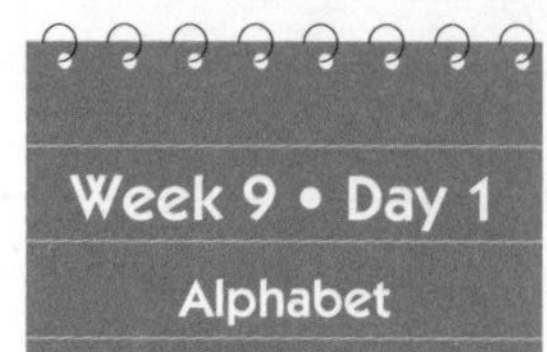

Letter X

Trace and write.

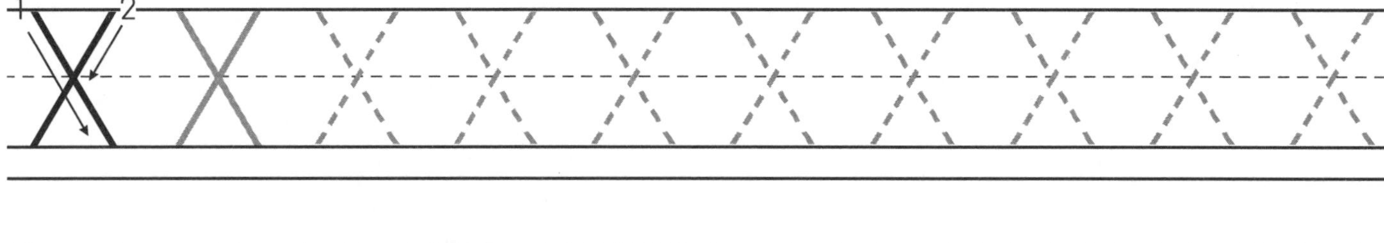

Circle every **X** and every **x**.

Y X K X K X X Y

x k y k x y g k

I found _____ X's and _____ x's.

Add x's and then read the words.

	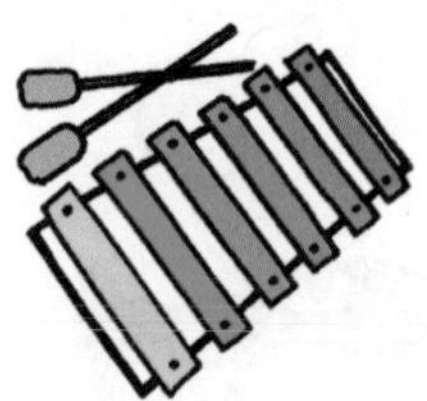	
fo ____	____ ylophone	____ -ray

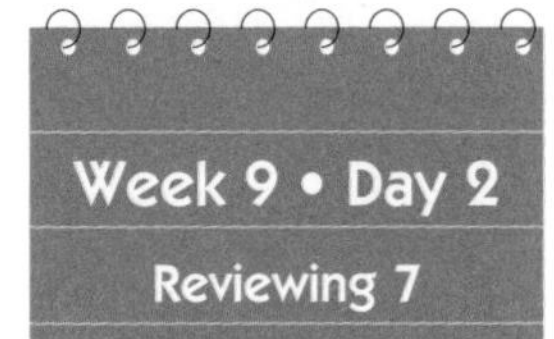

Number Practice: 7

Trace the number.

7

Write the number.

Trace the word.

Write the word.

Number Hunt

Circle every number 7.

5	7	1	8	13	9	25	7	4	26
11	5	7	12	3	25	3	9	8	1
2	16	24	3	7	5	4	3	20	0
8	7	29	1	3	7	19	8	10	14

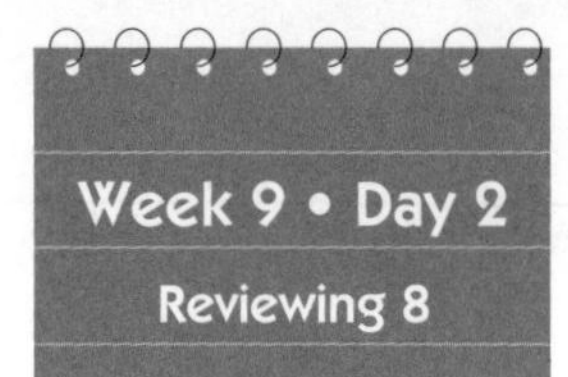

Number Practice: 8

Trace the number.

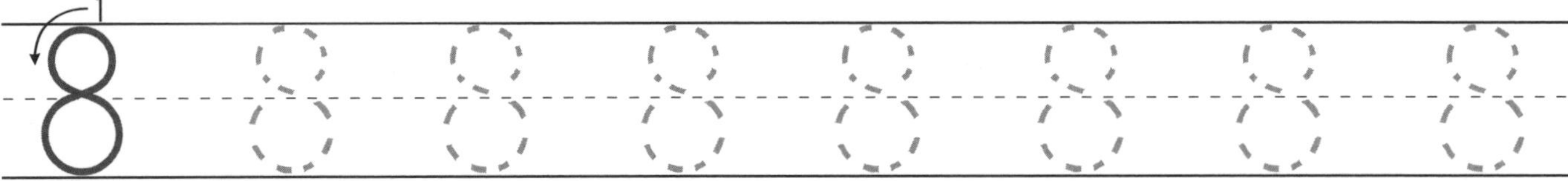

Write the number.

Trace the word.

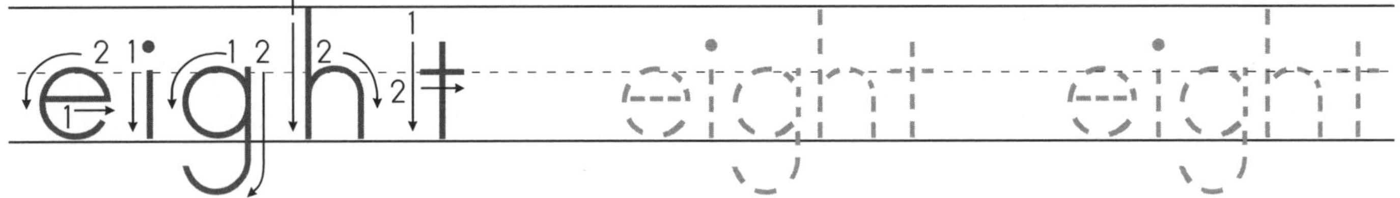

Write the word.

Number Hunt

Circle every number 8.

9	25	2	4	26	8	13	4	0	8
12	3	25	3	9	21	5	7	8	1
24	8	0	5	4	3	20	0	5	8
1	8	7	19	8	10	14	9	3	0

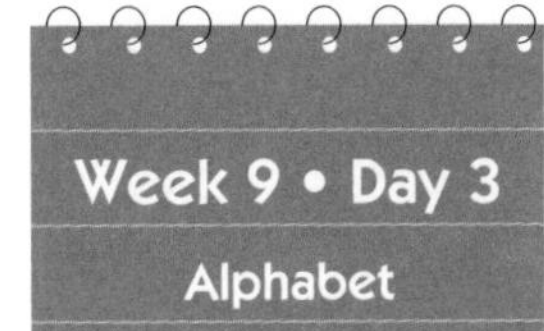

Letter Y

Trace and write.

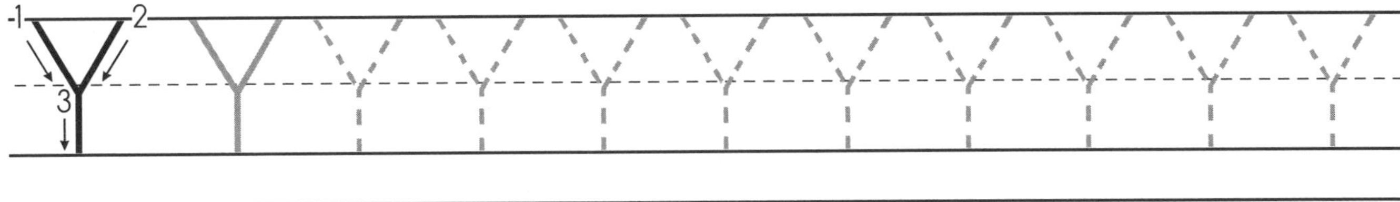

Circle every **Y** and every **y**.

U Y U V Y V Y U

y g x j y j g j

I found ______ Y's and ______ y's.

Add y's and then read the words.

 ____ arn	 ____ ard	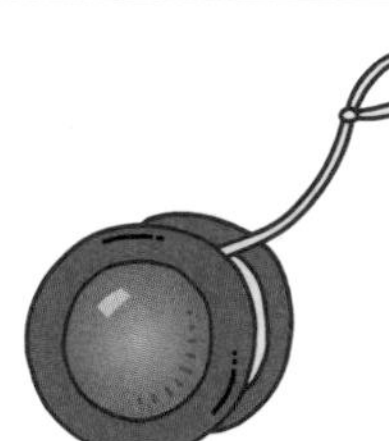 ____ o-yo

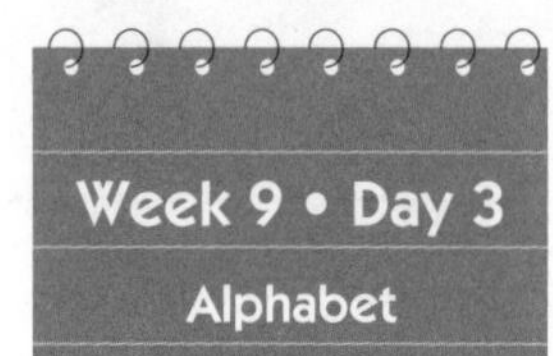

Letter Z

Trace and write.

1 → Z 2 3 →

1 → z 2 3 →

Circle every **Z** and every **z**.

Z X Y S Z S X Z

z s x k z c s z

I found ______ Z's and ______ z's.

Add z's and then read the words.

		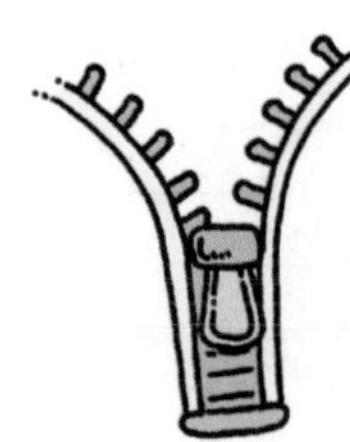
______ ebra	______ ero	______ ipper

Together Is Better

Circle the picture that goes with the first picture in each row.

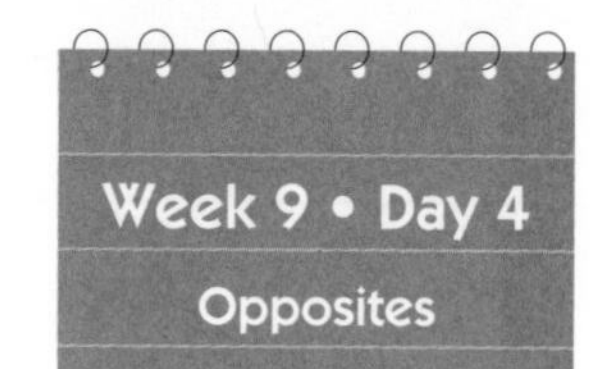

Different as Can Be

Follow the maze to match the pictures that show the opposite.

Time for Rhymes

Rhyming words have the same ending sound.

Say the name of each picture. Circle the two pictures that rhyme in each group.

You Can Draw a Dinosaur!

1 Draw a small circle for the head.	2 Draw a large oval for the body.	3 Connect the head and body with two lines.
4 Draw a curved triangle for the tail.	5 Draw four rectangles for legs.	6 Add facial features, spots, and toes.

____________________'s Incentive Chart: Week 10

Name Here

This week, I plan to read __________ minutes each day.

CHART YOUR PROGRESS HERE.

Week 1	Day 1	Day 2	Day 3	Day 4	Day 5
I read for...	minutes	minutes	minutes	minutes	minutes
Put a sticker to show you completed each day's work.					

Congratulations!

Wow! You did a great job this week!

#1

Place sticker here.

Parent or Caregiver's Signature ______________________________

Number Practice: 9

Trace the number.

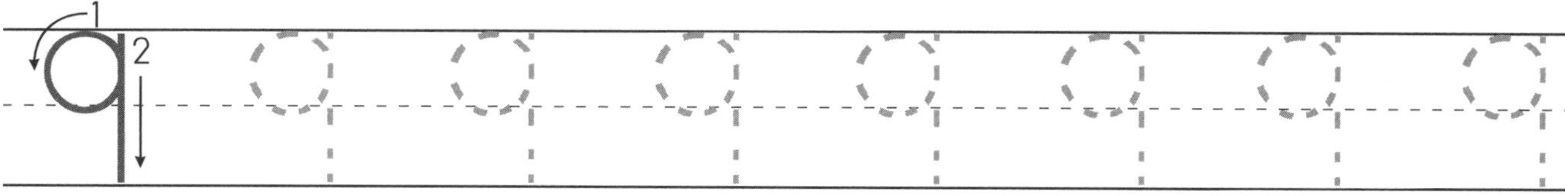

Write the number.

Trace the word.

Write the word.

Number Hunt

Circle every number 9.

9	3	1	8	13	9	25	2	4	26
8	1	2	21	5	7	12	3	25	3
0	9	4	3	20	0	9	8	16	24
1	7	20	8	10	3	0	2	9	14

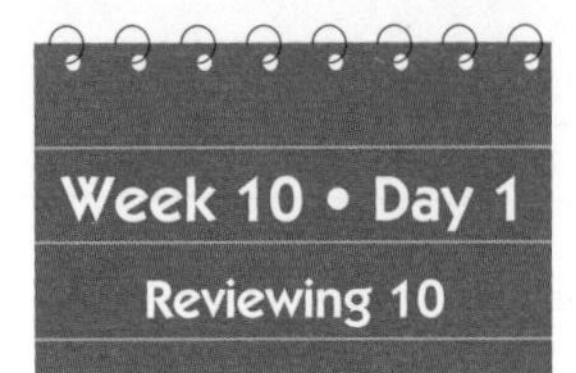

Number Practice: 10

Trace the number.

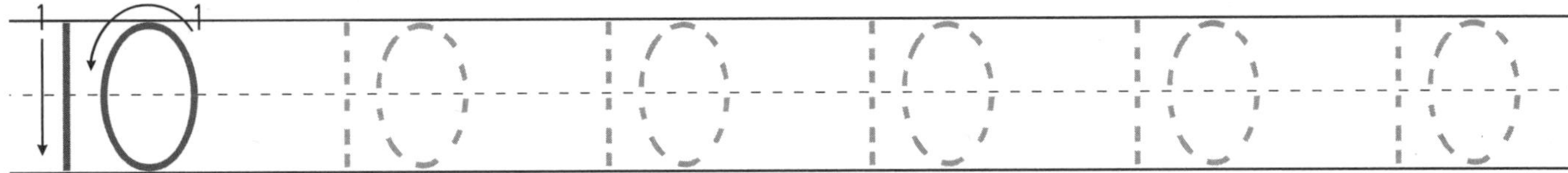

Write the number.

Trace the word.

Write the word.

Number Hunt

Circle every number 10.

2	4	26	40	3	1	8	10	9	25
10	25	3	9	8	1	2	21	5	7
3	0	5	4	3	10	0	5	8	10
7	10	8	10	14	9	3	0	29	1

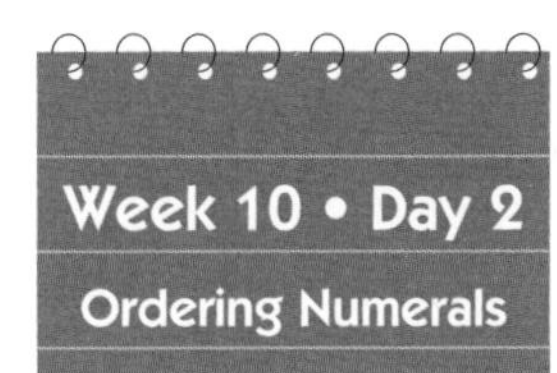

Crawl Before You Fly

Write the missing numbers.

Connect the dots from **1** to **10**.

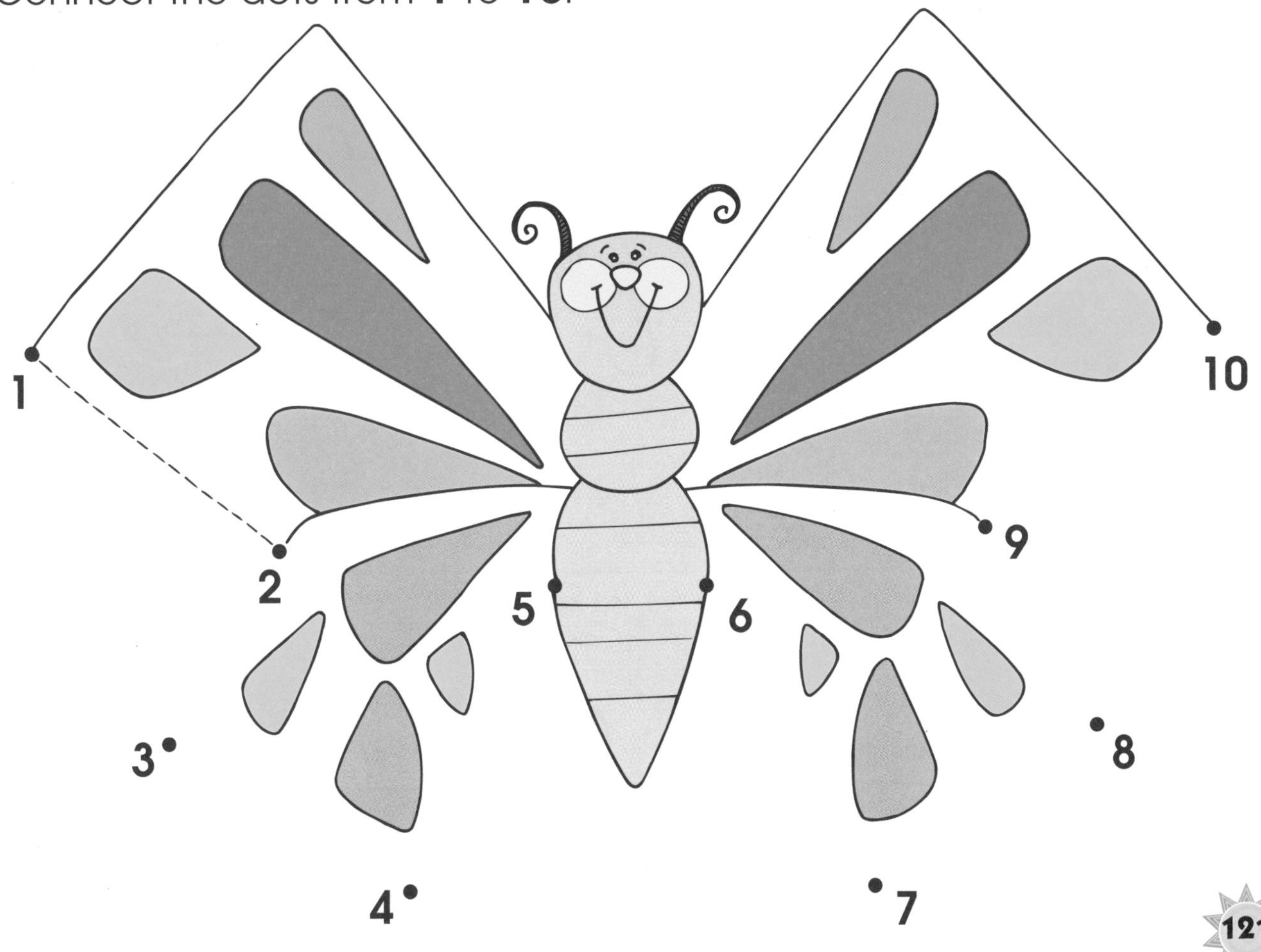

1
2
3
4
5
6
7
8
9
10

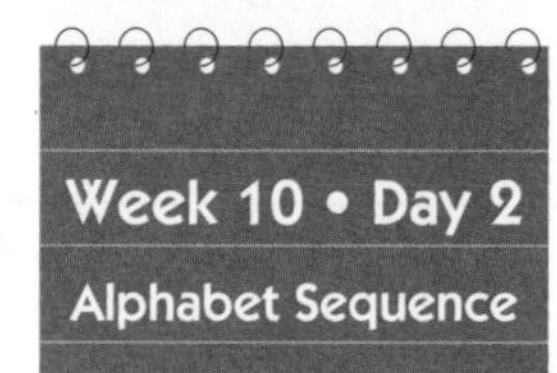

ABC Picture

Connect the dots in ABC order to find the hidden picture.
Tell a story about the picture.

H G B C A F D E K Z L I Y N J V M X U O P W T Q R S

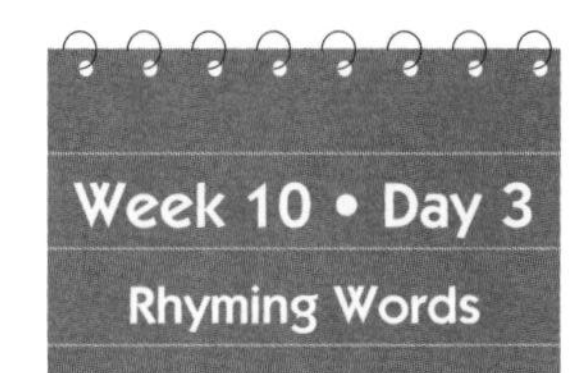

Rhyme Time

Rhyming words have the same ending sound.

Say the name of each picture. Circle the two pictures that rhyme in each row.

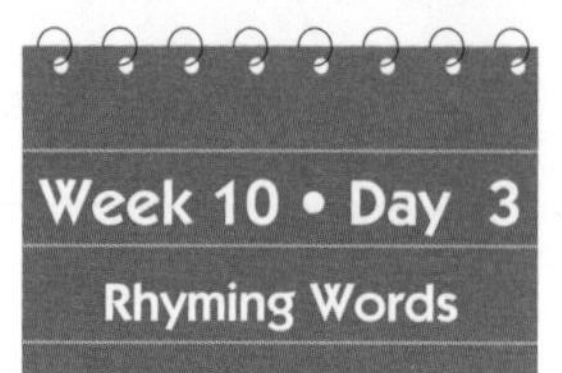

Check the Signs

Say the name of each picture. Circle the animal with the picture that rhymes with the first picture in each row.

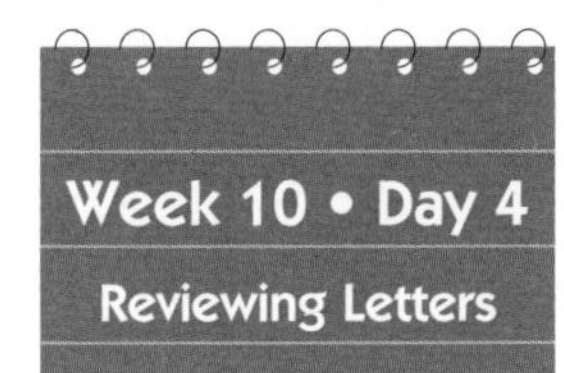

Matching Letters

Read the letter of the alphabet next to the number in each row. Find a letter that is just the same in that row. Fill in the circle in front of that letter.

1. A ○ C ○ A ○ B ○ H
2. D ○ D ○ L ○ P ○ U
3. K ○ F ○ C ○ H ○ K
4. M ○ N ○ G ○ M ○ A
5. T ○ E ○ T ○ O ○ I
6. s ○ i ○ s ○ r ○ c
7. e ○ u ○ t ○ e ○ s
8. b ○ t ○ b ○ c ○ p
9. n ○ h ○ m ○ o ○ n
10. z ○ z ○ h ○ s ○ a

Show What You Know

1. Which one is the same?

2. Which one is different?

3. Which animal name begins with the same sound?

4. Which animal name rhymes?

Oh no! There they go!

Picking Letters

I have Q, R, S, and T.

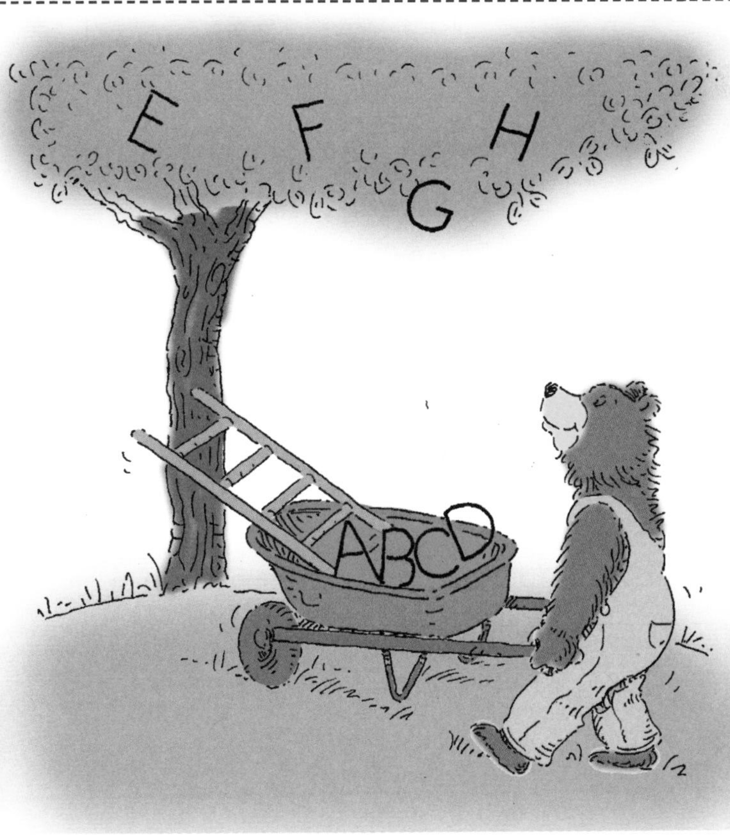

I have E, F, G, and H.

I have A, B, C, and D.

2

I have U, V, W, and X, Y, Z.

7

I have I, J, K, and L.

4

I have M, N, O, and P.

5

Answer Key

Week 1

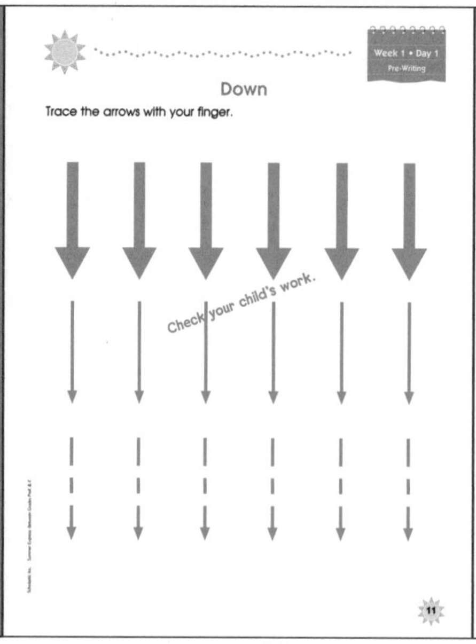

Week 1 • Day 1
Pre-Writing
Down
Trace the arrows with your finger.
Check your child's work.
11

page 11

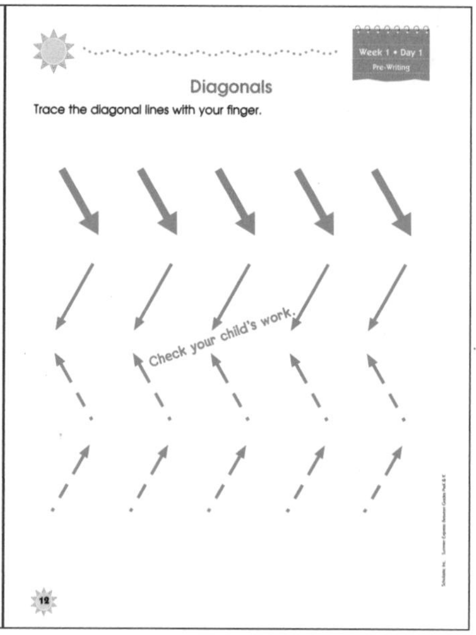

Week 1 • Day 1
Pre-Writing
Diagonals
Trace the diagonal lines with your finger.
Check your child's work.
12

page 12

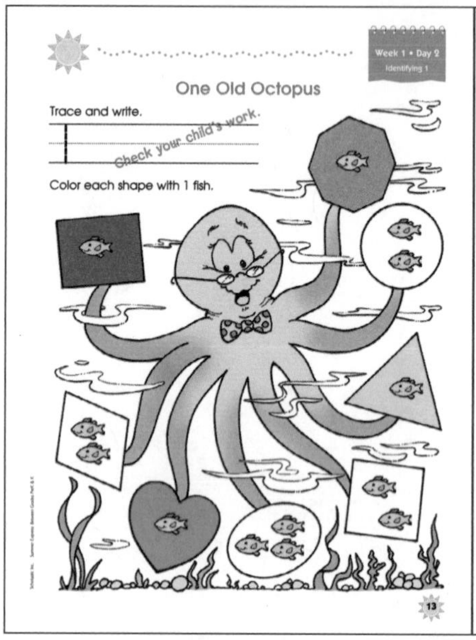

Week 1 • Day 2
Identifying 1
One Old Octopus
Trace and write.
Check your child's work.
Color each shape with 1 fish.
13

page 13

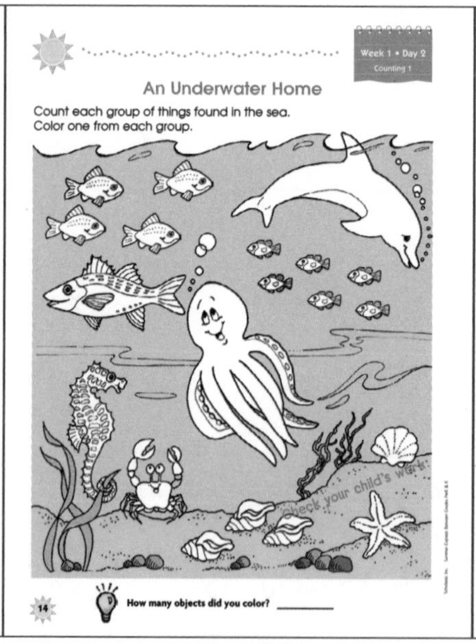

Week 1 • Day 2
Counting 1
An Underwater Home
Count each group of things found in the sea.
Color one from each group.
Check your child's work.
14
How many objects did you color?

page 14

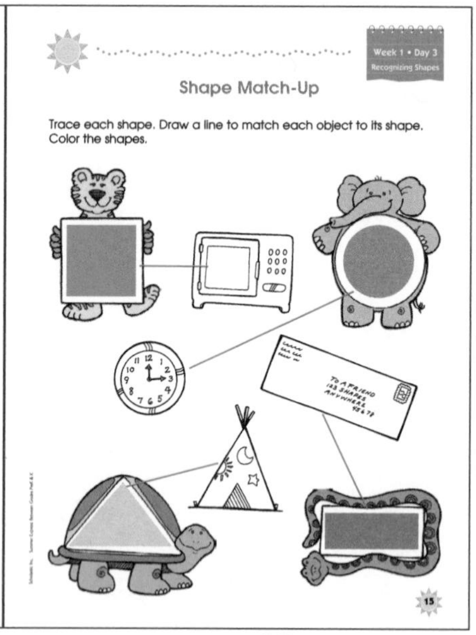

Week 1 • Day 3
Recognizing Shapes
Shape Match-Up
Trace each shape. Draw a line to match each object to its shape.
Color the shapes.
15

page 15

Week 1 • Day 3
Identifying Colors
Clowning Around
Color the picture below.
yellow
green
purple
red
blue
black
orange
16

page 16

Week 1 • Day 4
Pre-Writing
Curves
Trace the arrows with your finger.
Check your child's work.
17

page 17

Week 1 • Day 4
Pre-Writing
Circles
Trace the arrows with your finger.
Check your child's work.
18

page 18

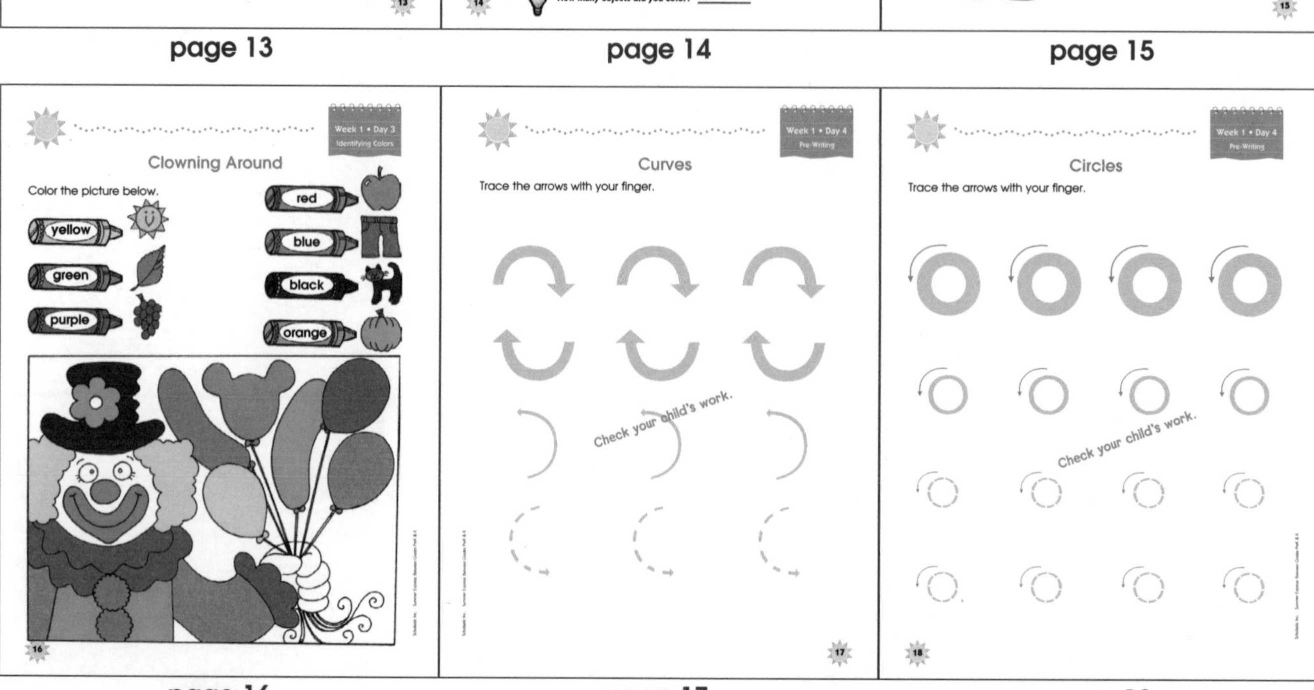

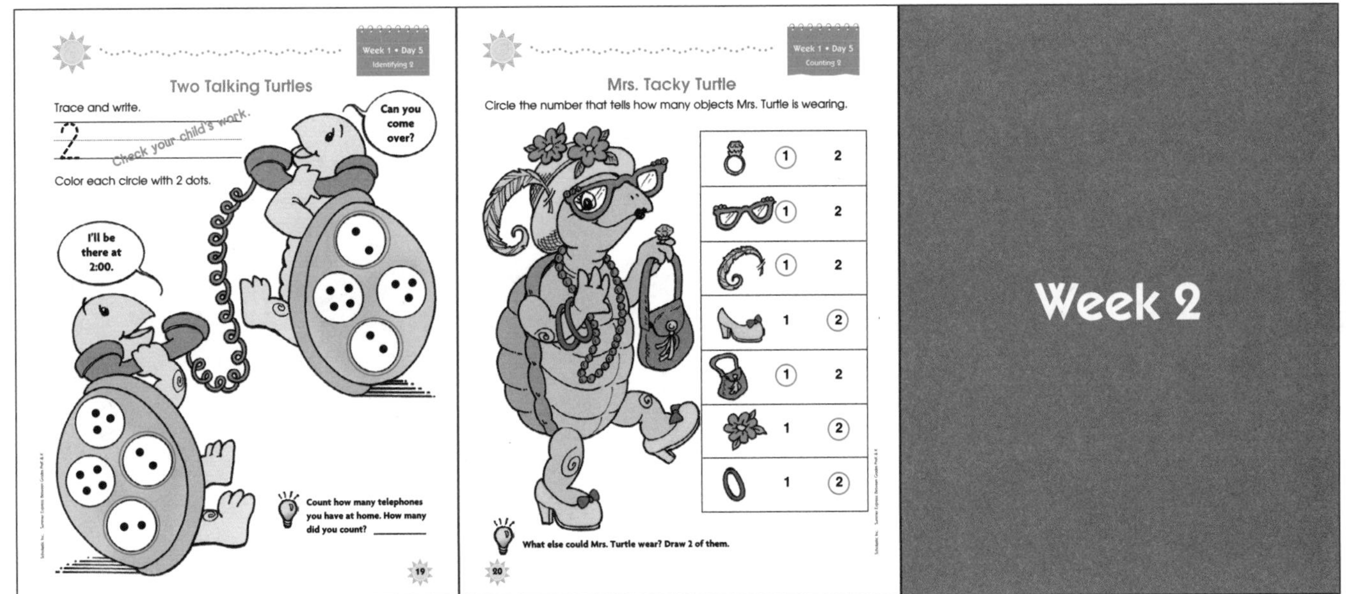

page 19

page 20

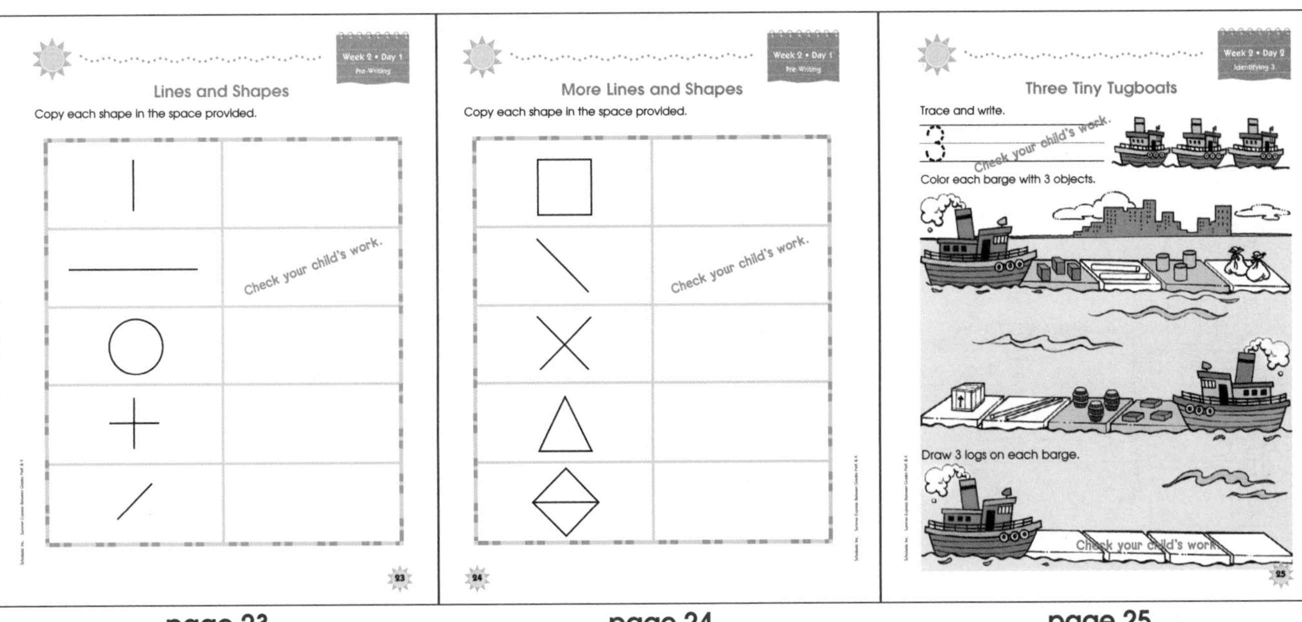

page 23

page 24

page 25

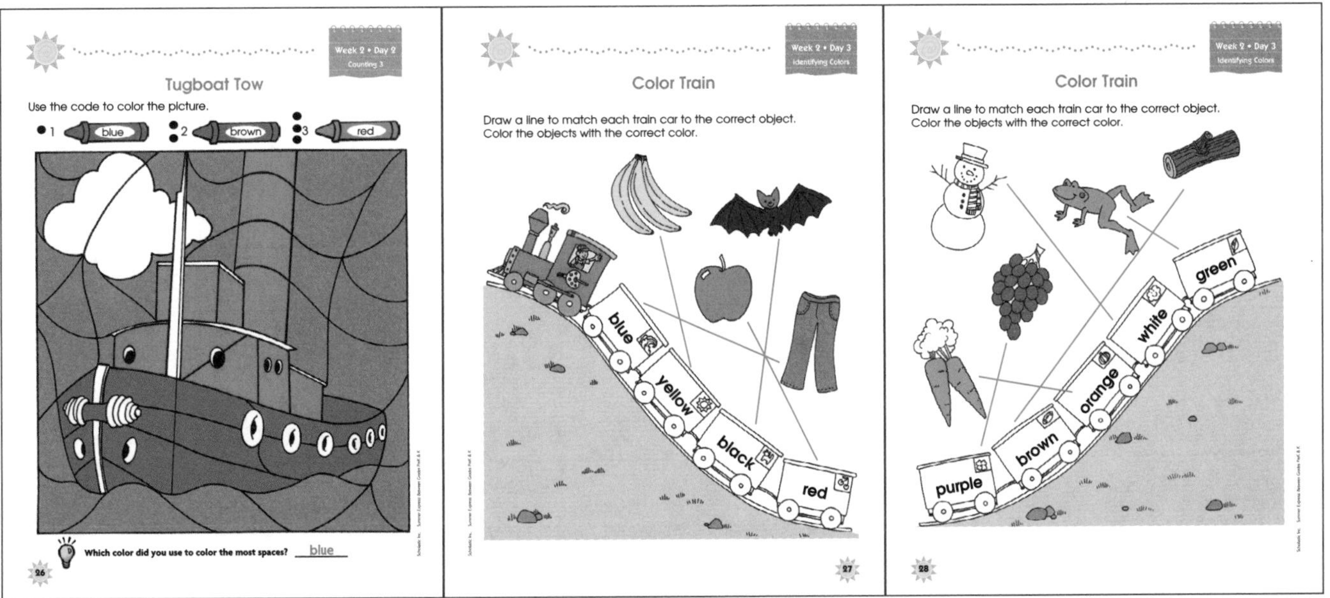

page 26

page 27

page 28

Week 2 • Day 4
Identifying 4

Four Fine Firefighters

Trace and write.

Check your child's work.

Color each dog with 4 spots.

29

page 29

Week 2 • Day 4
Counting 4

Climb to the Top

Count the objects on each step.
Circle the matching number.

How many steps have 4 objects? 3

30

page 30

Week 2 • Day 5
Recognizing Shapes

Sorting Shapes

This is a **circle**. This is a **square**. A square has four sides that are the same length. This is a **rectangle**. A rectangle also has four sides. The opposite sides of a rectangle are the same length. This is a **triangle**. A triangle has three sides.

Color the circles yellow.
Color the squares red.
Color the triangles green.
Color the rectangles blue.

31

page 31

Week 2 • Day 5
Vocabulary

Going to School

Find and color these things in the picture.

pencil scissors book
paper glue eraser

Put an X on one thing in the picture that does not belong.

32

page 32

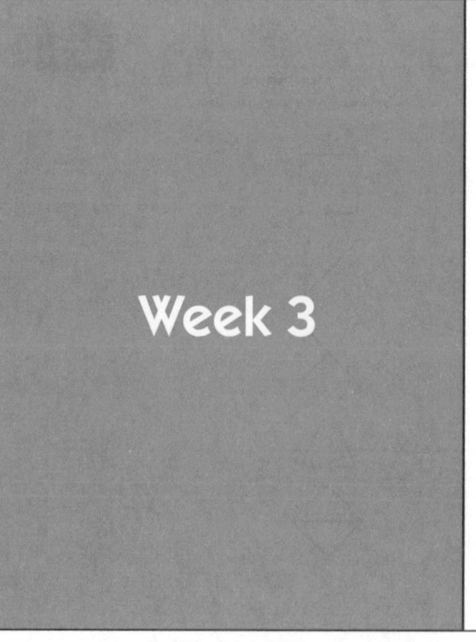

Week 3

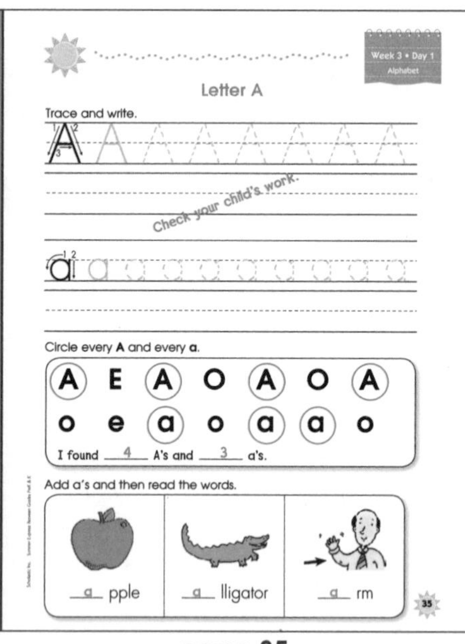

Week 3 • Day 1
Alphabet

Letter A

Trace and write.

Check your child's work.

Circle every **A** and every **a**.

A E A O A O A
o e a o a a o

I found 4 A's and 3 a's.

Add a's and then read the words.

a pple
a lligator
a rm

35

page 35

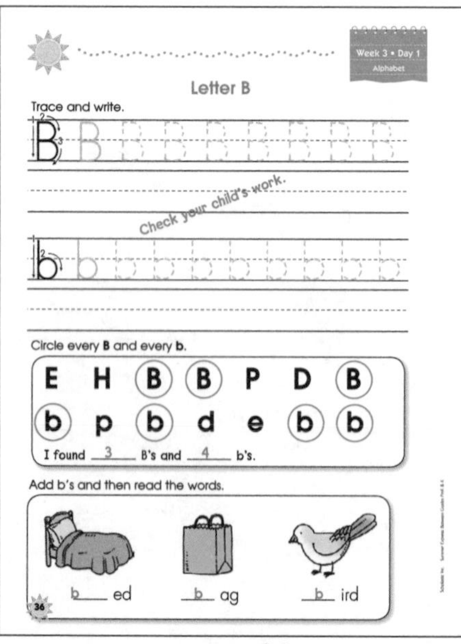

Week 3 • Day 1
Alphabet

Letter B

Trace and write.

Check your child's work.

Circle every **B** and every **b**.

E H B B P D B
b p b d e b b

I found 3 B's and 4 b's.

Add b's and then read the words.

b ed
b ag
b ird

36

page 36

Week 3 • Day 2
Identifying 5

Five Friendly Frogs

Trace and write.

Check your child's work.

Color each lily pad with 5 flies.

37

page 37

Week 3 • Day 2
Counting 5

Fast Frogs

Circle each rock with 5 bugs to find which frog finishes first.

How many rocks have 5 bugs? 14

38

page 38

Week 3 • Day 3
Recognizing Shapes
A Shapely Castle
Color the shapes in the picture below using the code.
yellow
purple
blue
green
orange
red

page 39

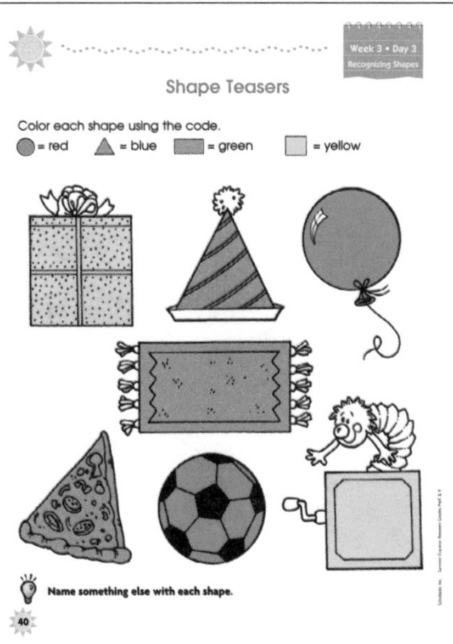
Week 3 • Day 3
Recognizing Shapes
Shape Teasers
Color each shape using the code.
= red
= blue
= green
= yellow
Name something else with each shape.

page 40

Week 3 • Day 4
Identifying 6
Six Smelly Shoes
Trace and write.
Check your child's work.
Circle 6 shoes in each box.
Draw more shoes to make 6.
Check your child's work.
Count the socks. Circle the right number. 5 6 7

page 41

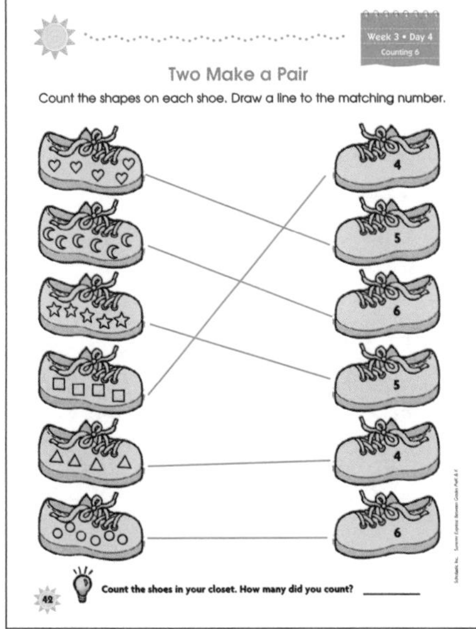
Week 3 • Day 4
Counting 6
Two Make a Pair
Count the shapes on each shoe. Draw a line to the matching number.
4
5
6
5
4
6
Count the shoes in your closet. How many did you count?

page 42

Week 3 • Day 5
More Than/Less Than
Tricks for Treats
Count the bones each dog has. In each box, circle the dog with less bones.

page 43

Week 3 • Day 1
Opposites
Just the Right Size
This butterfly is large.
This butterfly is small.
Circle the large picture on each petal.
Name two things that are larger than you.

page 44

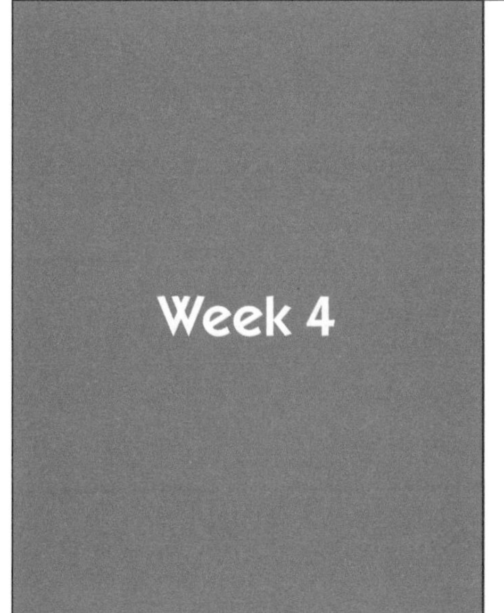
Week 4

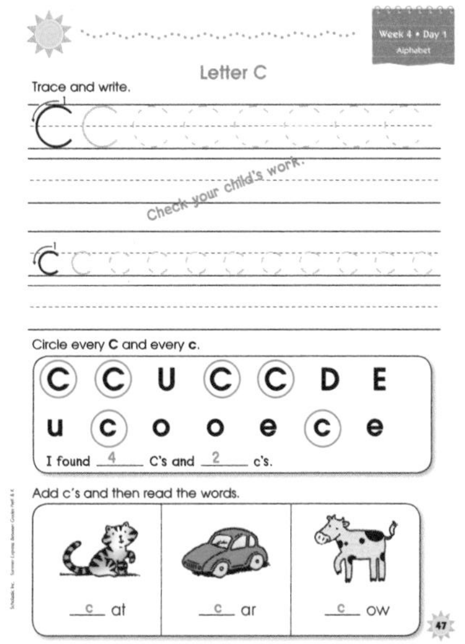
Week 4 • Day 1
Alphabet
Letter C
Trace and write.
Check your child's work.
Circle every C and every c.
C C U C C D E
u c o o e c e
I found 4 C's and 2 c's.
Add c's and then read the words.
c at
c ar
c ow

page 47

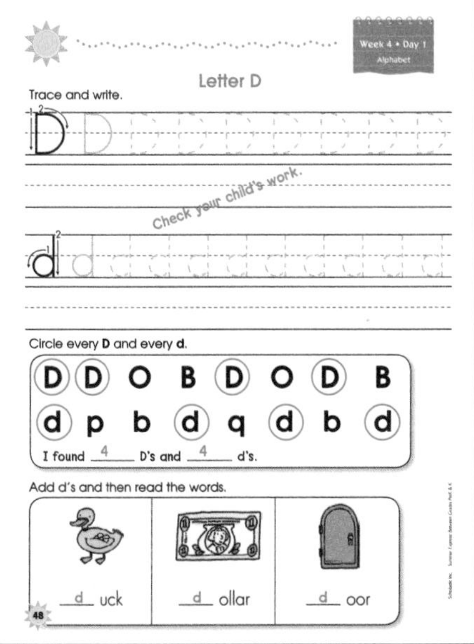
Week 4 • Day 1
Alphabet
Letter D
Trace and write.
Check your child's work.
Circle every D and every d.
D D O B D O D B
d p b d q d b d
I found 4 D's and 4 d's.
Add d's and then read the words.
d uck
d ollar
d oor

page 48

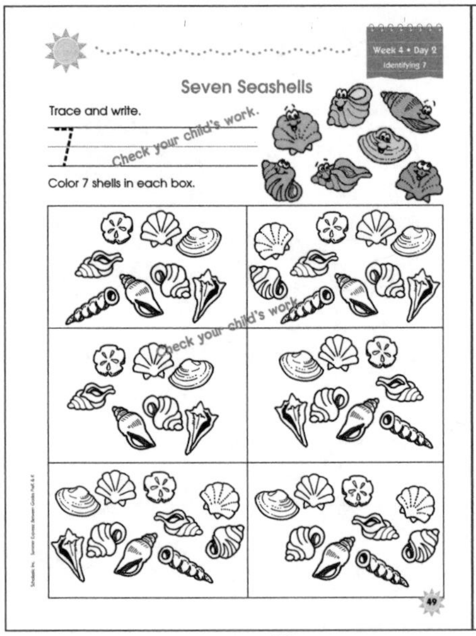

Week 4 • Day 2
Identifying 7

Seven Seashells

Trace and write.

7

Check your child's work.

Color 7 shells in each box.

Check your child's work.

49

page 49

Week 4 • Day 2
Counting 7

Seashells by the Seashore

Count each kind of shell in the picture. Write the total number next to the correct shell. Circle the shells that total 7.

4 7
5 7

Circle the number that tells how many.

6 (7)	(6) 7
(6) 7	6 (7)

50

page 50

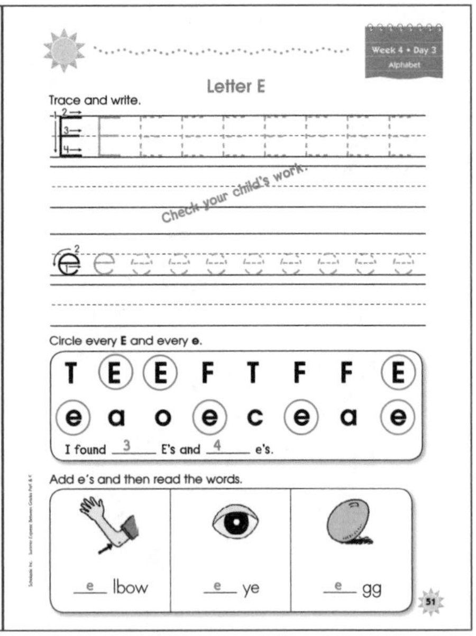

Week 4 • Day 3
Alphabet

Letter E

Trace and write.

E

Check your child's work.

e

Circle every **E** and every **e**.

T (E) (E) F T F F (E)

(e) a o (e) c (e) a (e)

I found 3 E's and 4 e's.

Add e's and then read the words.

e lbow	e ye	e gg

51

page 51

Week 4 • Day 3
Alphabet

Letter F

Trace and write.

F

Check your child's work.

f

Circle every **F** and every **f**.

(F) E T (F) E E (F) T

(f) t t (f) l (f) k (f)

I found 3 F's and 4 f's.

Add f's and then read the words.

f eather	f ish	f ork

52

page 52

Week 4 • Day 4
Identifying 8

Eight Electric Eels

Trace and write.

8

Check your child's work.

Draw more eels to make 8.

Check your child's work.

Count the eels. Color the animal with the matching number.

7 8 9

53

page 53

Week 4 • Day 4
Counting 8

Eddie Eel Is Lost

Help Eddie Eel find his way back to the cave. Trace the path that goes in order from 1 to 8.

1 2 3 4 5 6 7 8

On a sheet of paper, draw a picture of 8 different sea creatures.

54

page 54

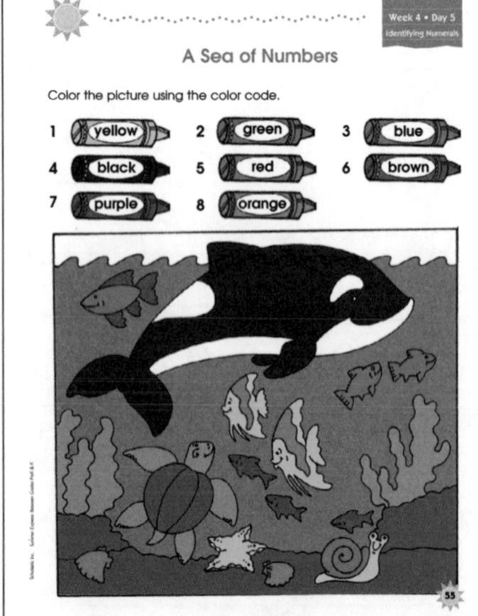

page 55

page 56

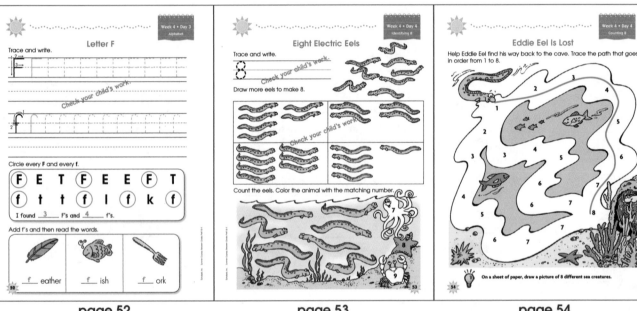

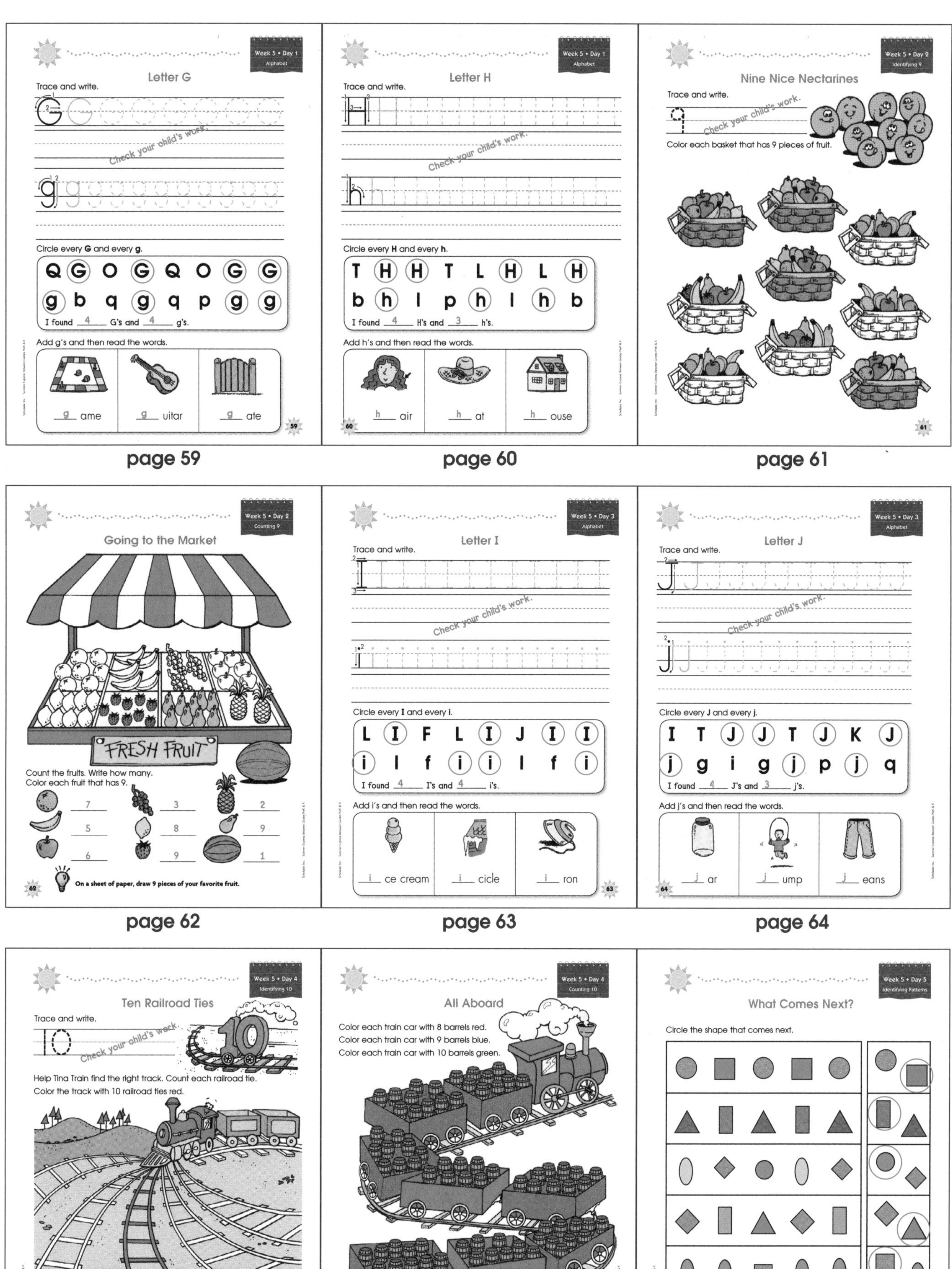

page 59 page 60 page 61

page 62 page 63 page 64

page 65 page 66 page 67

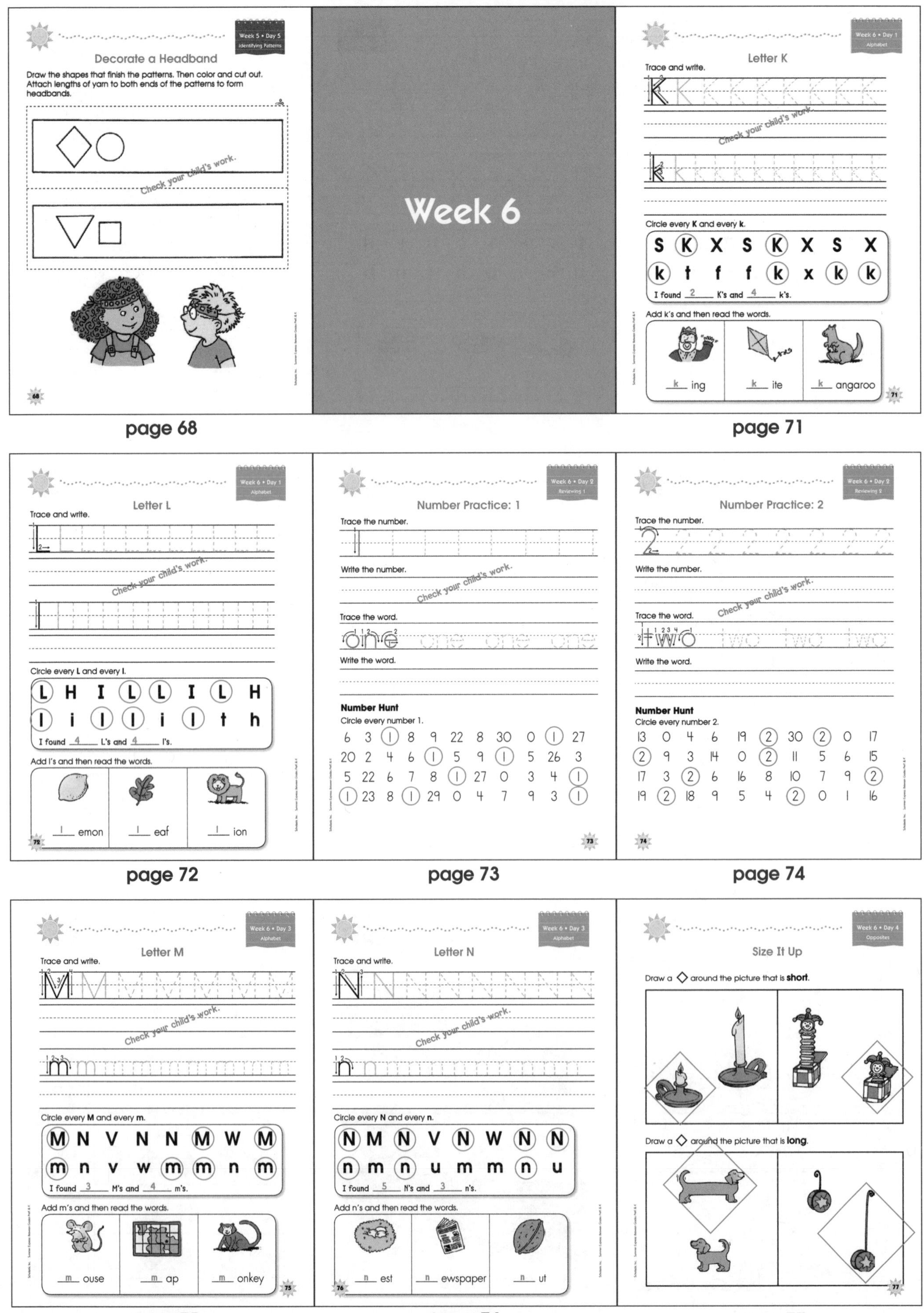

Week 5 • Day 5
Identifying Patterns

Decorate a Headband

Draw the shapes that finish the patterns. Then color and cut out. Attach lengths of yarn to both ends of the patterns to form headbands.

Check your child's work.

68

page 68

Week 6

Week 6 • Day 1
Alphabet

Letter K

Trace and write.

Check your child's work.

Circle every K and every k.

S K X S K X S X

k t f f k x k k

I found 2 K's and 4 k's.

Add k's and then read the words.

k ing | k ite | k angaroo

71

page 71

Week 6 • Day 1
Alphabet

Letter L

Trace and write.

Check your child's work.

Circle every L and every l.

L H I L L I L H

l i l l i l t h

I found 4 L's and 4 l's.

Add l's and then read the words.

l emon | l eaf | l ion

72

page 72

Week 6 • Day 2
Reviewing 1

Number Practice: 1

Trace the number.

Write the number.

Check your child's work.

Trace the word.

one one one one

Write the word.

Number Hunt

Circle every number 1.

6 3 1 8 9 22 8 30 0 1 27

20 2 4 6 1 5 9 1 5 26 3

5 22 6 7 8 1 27 0 3 4 1

1 23 8 1 29 0 4 7 9 3 1

73

page 73

Week 6 • Day 2
Reviewing 2

Number Practice: 2

Trace the number.

Write the number.

Check your child's work.

Trace the word.

two two two two

Write the word.

Number Hunt

Circle every number 2.

13 0 4 6 19 2 30 2 0 17

2 9 3 14 0 2 11 5 6 15

17 3 2 6 16 8 10 7 9 2

19 2 18 9 5 4 2 0 1 16

74

page 74

Week 6 • Day 3
Alphabet

Letter M

Trace and write.

Check your child's work.

Circle every M and every m.

M N V N N M W M

m n v w m m n m

I found 3 M's and 4 m's.

Add m's and then read the words.

m ouse | m ap | m onkey

75

page 75

Week 6 • Day 3
Alphabet

Letter N

Trace and write.

Check your child's work.

Circle every N and every n.

N M N V N W N N

n m n u m m n u

I found 5 N's and 3 n's.

Add n's and then read the words.

n est | n ewspaper | n ut

76

page 76

Week 6 • Day 4
Opposites

Size It Up

Draw a ◇ around the picture that is **short**.

Draw a ◇ around the picture that is **long**.

77

page 77

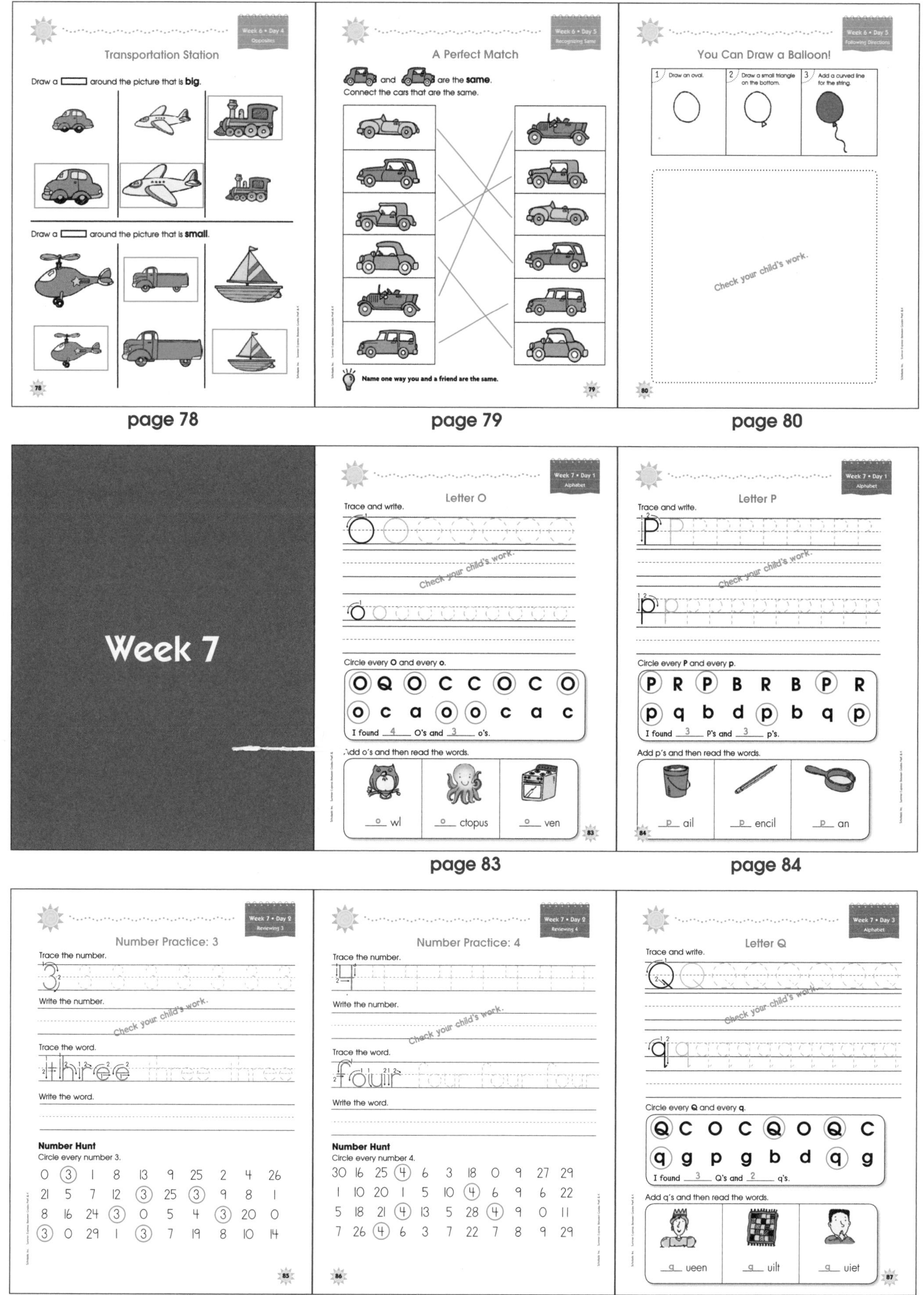

Week 6 • Day 4
Opposites

Transportation Station

Draw a ▭ around the picture that is **big**.

Draw a ▭ around the picture that is **small**.

78

page 78

Week 6 • Day 5
Recognizing Same

A Perfect Match

and are the **same**.
Connect the cars that are the same.

Name one way you and a friend are the same.

79

page 79

Week 6 • Day 5
Following Directions

You Can Draw a Balloon!

1 Draw an oval.
2 Draw a small triangle on the bottom.
3 Add a curved line for the string.

Check your child's work.

80

page 80

Week 7

Week 7 • Day 1
Alphabet

Letter O

Trace and write.

Check your child's work.

Circle every **O** and every **o**.

(O) Q (O) C C (O) C (O)

(o) c a (o) (o) c a c

I found 4 O's and 3 o's.

Add o's and then read the words.

o wl | o ctopus | o ven

83

page 83

Week 7 • Day 1
Alphabet

Letter P

Trace and write.

Check your child's work.

Circle every **P** and every **p**.

(P) R (P) B R B (P) R

(p) q b d (p) b q (p)

I found 3 P's and 3 p's.

Add p's and then read the words.

p ail | p encil | p an

84

page 84

Week 7 • Day 2
Reviewing 3

Number Practice: 3

Trace the number.

Write the number.

Check your child's work.

Trace the word.

three three three

Write the word.

Number Hunt
Circle every number 3.

0 (3) 1 8 13 9 25 2 4 26
21 5 7 12 (3) 25 (3) 9 8 1
8 16 24 (3) 0 5 4 (3) 20 0
(3) 0 29 1 (3) 7 19 8 10 14

85

page 85

Week 7 • Day 2
Reviewing 4

Number Practice: 4

Trace the number.

Write the number.

Check your child's work.

Trace the word.

four four four four

Write the word.

Number Hunt
Circle every number 4.

30 16 25 (4) 6 3 18 0 9 27 29
1 10 20 1 5 10 (4) 6 9 6 22
5 18 21 (4) 13 5 28 (4) 9 0 11
7 26 (4) 6 3 7 22 7 8 9 29

86

page 86

Week 7 • Day 3
Alphabet

Letter Q

Trace and write.

Check your child's work.

Circle every **Q** and every **q**.

(Q) C O C (Q) O (Q) C

(q) g p g b d (q) g

I found 3 Q's and 2 q's.

Add q's and then read the words.

q ueen | q uilt | q uiet

87

page 87

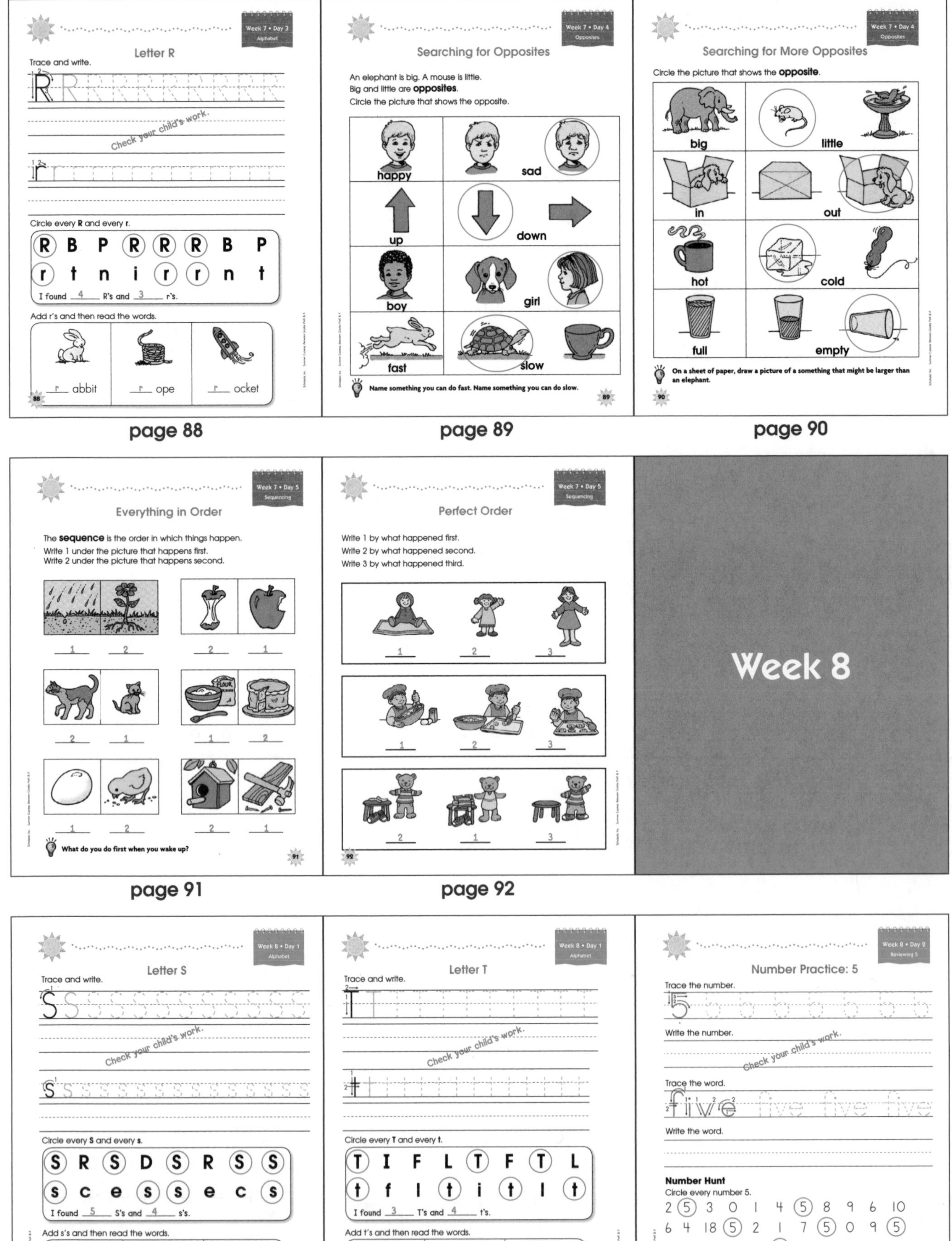

Week 7 • Day 3 Alphabet

Letter R

Trace and write.

Check your child's work.

Circle every **R** and every **r**.

R B P R R R B P

r t n i r r n t

I found 4 R's and 3 r's.

Add r's and then read the words.

r abbit r ope r ocket

88

page 88

Week 7 • Day 4 Opposites

Searching for Opposites

An elephant is big. A mouse is little.
Big and little are **opposites**.
Circle the picture that shows the opposite.

happy sad
up down
boy girl
fast slow

Name something you can do fast. Name something you can do slow.

89

page 89

Week 7 • Day 4 Opposites

Searching for More Opposites

Circle the picture that shows the **opposite**.

big little
in out
hot cold
full empty

On a sheet of paper, draw a picture of a something that might be larger than an elephant.

90

page 90

Week 7 • Day 5 Sequencing

Everything in Order

The **sequence** is the order in which things happen.
Write 1 under the picture that happens first.
Write 2 under the picture that happens second.

1 2 2 1
2 1 1 2
1 2 2 1

What do you do first when you wake up?

91

page 91

Week 7 • Day 5 Sequencing

Perfect Order

Write 1 by what happened first.
Write 2 by what happened second.
Write 3 by what happened third.

1 2 3
1 2 3
2 1 3

92

page 92

Week 8

Week 8 • Day 1 Alphabet

Letter S

Trace and write.

Check your child's work.

Circle every **S** and every **s**.

S R S D S R S S

s c e s s e c s

I found 5 S's and 4 s's.

Add s's and then read the words.

s andwich s ock s oap

95

page 95

Week 8 • Day 1 Alphabet

Letter T

Trace and write.

Check your child's work.

Circle every **T** and every **t**.

T I F L T F T L

t f l t i t l t

I found 3 T's and 4 t's.

Add t's and then read the words.

t ent t oothbrush t ub

96

page 96

Week 8 • Day 2 Reviewing 5

Number Practice: 5

Trace the number.

Write the number.

Check your child's work.

Trace the word.

five five five five

Write the word.

Number Hunt

Circle every number 5.

2 5 3 0 1 4 5 8 9 6 10

6 4 18 5 2 1 7 5 0 9 5

7 3 8 1 9 5 16 7 0 1 4

11 4 5 9 21 3 9 2 1 10 8

97

page 97

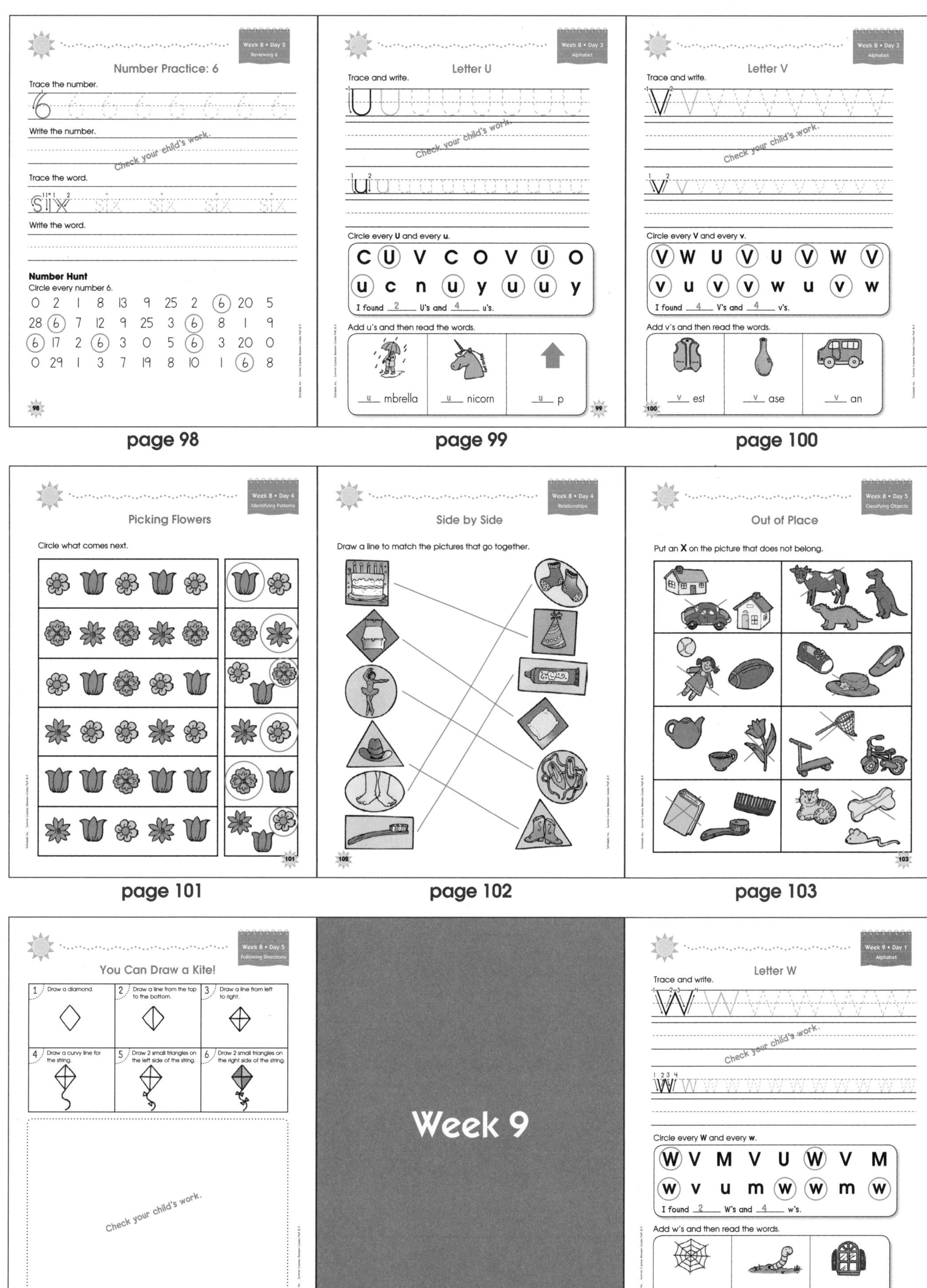

page 98 page 99 page 100

page 101 page 102 page 103

page 104 page 107

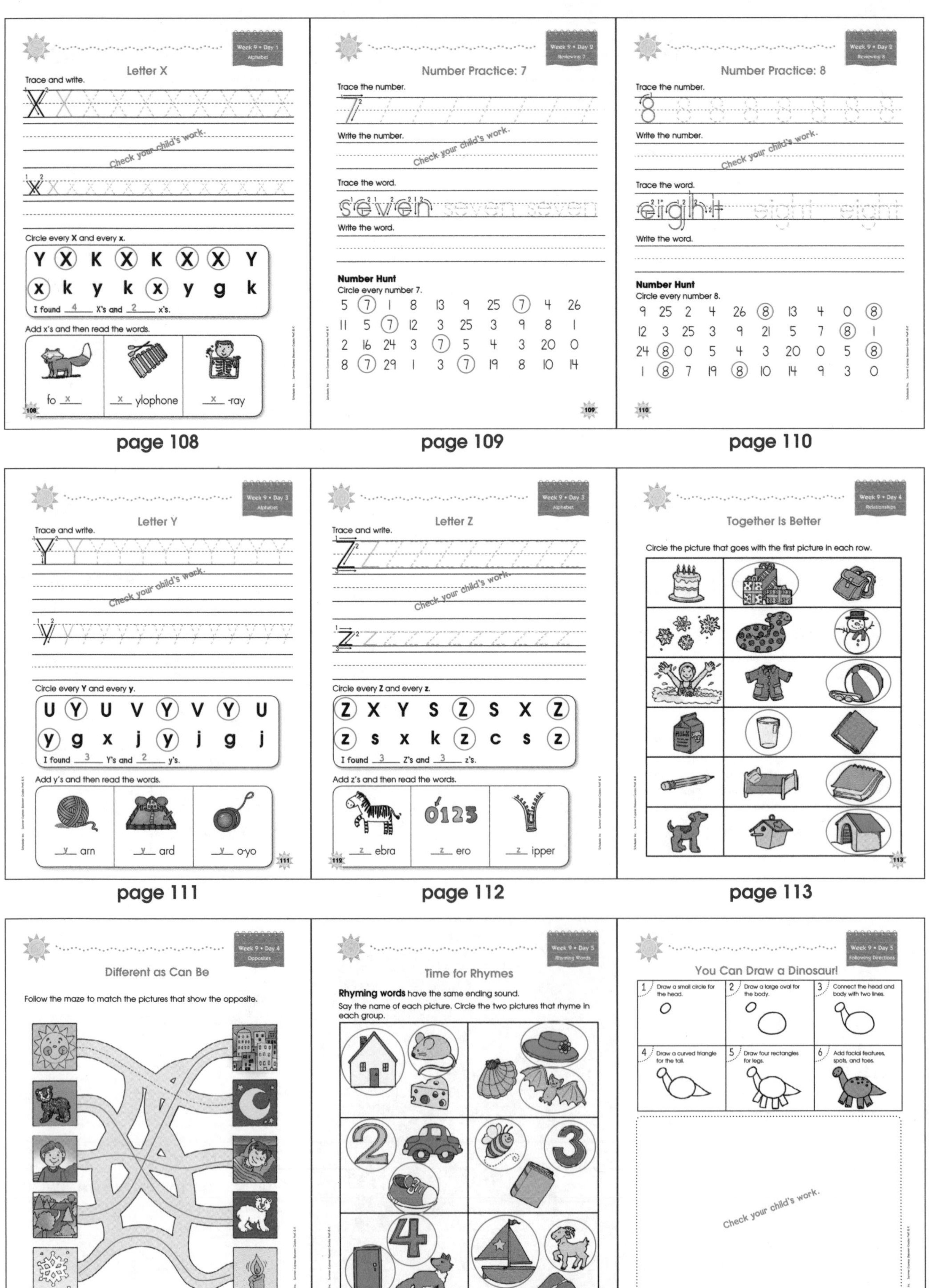
Week 9 • Day 1 Alphabet
Letter X
Trace and write.
Check your child's work.
Circle every X and every x.
Y X K X K X X Y
x k y k x y g k
I found 4 X's and 2 x's.
Add x's and then read the words.
fo x
x ylophone
x -ray
108
page 108
Week 9 • Day 2 Reviewing 7
Number Practice: 7
Trace the number.
Write the number.
Check your child's work.
Trace the word.
seven seven seven
Write the word.
Number Hunt
Circle every number 7.
5 7 1 8 13 9 25 7 4 26
11 5 7 12 3 25 3 9 8 1
2 16 24 3 7 5 4 3 20 0
8 7 29 1 3 7 19 8 10 14
109
page 109
Week 9 • Day 2 Reviewing 8
Number Practice: 8
Trace the number.
Write the number.
Check your child's work.
Trace the word.
eight eight eight
Write the word.
Number Hunt
Circle every number 8.
9 25 2 4 26 8 13 4 0 8
12 3 25 3 9 21 5 7 8 1
24 8 0 5 4 3 20 0 5 8
1 8 7 19 8 10 14 9 3 0
110
page 110
Week 9 • Day 3 Alphabet
Letter Y
Trace and write.
Check your child's work.
Circle every Y and every y.
U Y U V Y V Y U
y g x j y j g j
I found 3 Y's and 2 y's.
Add y's and then read the words.
y arn
y ard
y o-yo
111
page 111
Week 9 • Day 3 Alphabet
Letter Z
Trace and write.
Check your child's work.
Circle every Z and every z.
Z X Y S Z S X Z
z s x k z c s z
I found 3 Z's and 3 z's.
Add z's and then read the words.
z ebra
z ero
z ipper
0123
112
page 112
Week 9 • Day 4 Relationships
Together Is Better
Circle the picture that goes with the first picture in each row.
113
page 113
Week 9 • Day 4 Opposites
Different as Can Be
Follow the maze to match the pictures that show the opposite.
114
page 114
Week 9 • Day 5 Rhyming Words
Time for Rhymes
Rhyming words have the same ending sound.
Say the name of each picture. Circle the two pictures that rhyme in each group.
2
3
4
115
page 115
Week 9 • Day 5 Following Directions
You Can Draw a Dinosaur!
1 Draw a small circle for the head.
2 Draw a large oval for the body.
3 Connect the head and body with two lines.
4 Draw a curved triangle for the tail.
5 Draw four rectangles for legs.
6 Add facial features, spots, and toes.
Check your child's work.
116
page 116

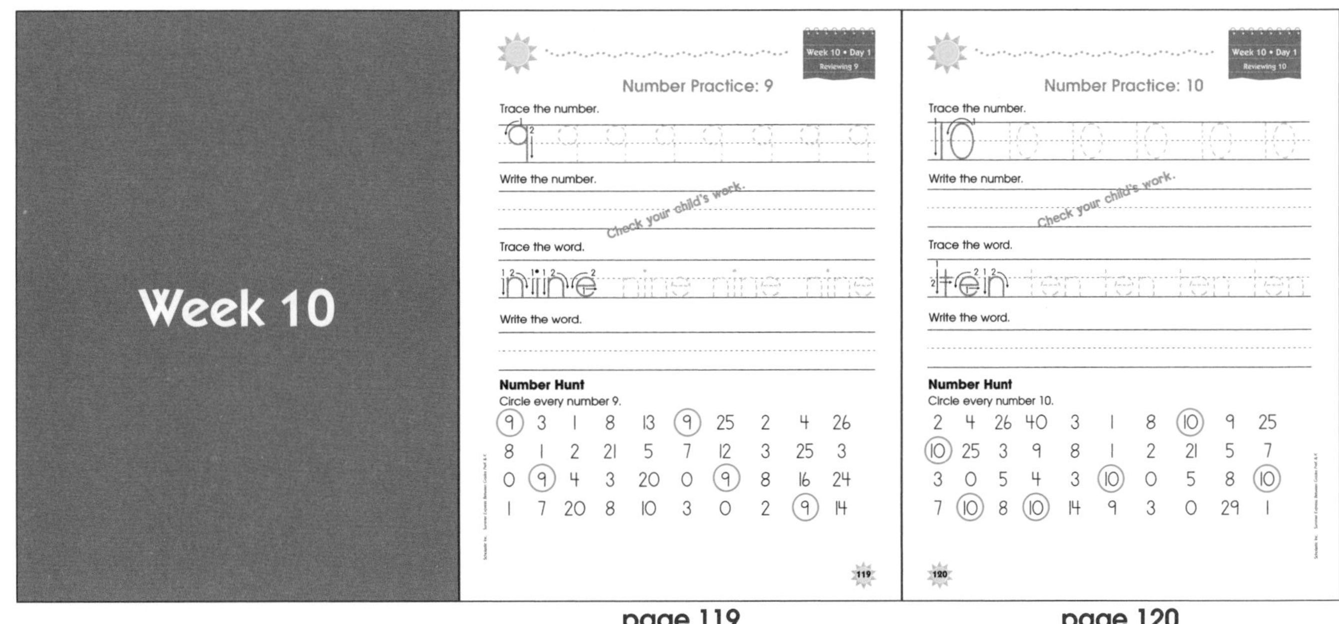

Week 10

Week 10 • Day 1
Reviewing 9

Number Practice: 9

Trace the number.

Write the number.

Check your child's work.

Trace the word.

nine nine nine nine

Write the word.

Number Hunt

Circle every number 9.

(9)	3	1	8	13	(9)	25	2	4	26
8	1	2	21	5	7	12	3	25	3
0	(9)	4	3	20	0	(9)	8	16	24
1	7	20	8	10	3	0	2	(9)	14

119

Week 10 • Day 1
Reviewing 10

Number Practice: 10

Trace the number.

Write the number.

Check your child's work.

Trace the word.

ten ten ten ten ten

Write the word.

Number Hunt

Circle every number 10.

2	4	26	40	3	1	8	(10)	9	25
(10)	25	3	9	8	1	2	21	5	7
3	0	5	4	3	(10)	0	5	8	(10)
7	(10)	8	(10)	14	9	3	0	29	1

120

page 119

page 120

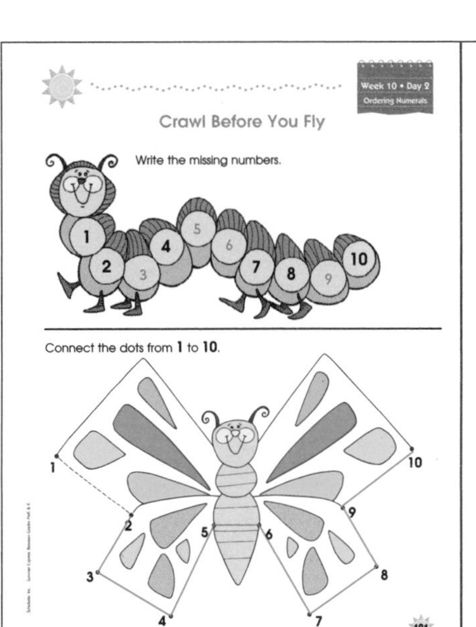

Week 10 • Day 2
Ordering Numerals

Crawl Before You Fly

Write the missing numbers.

1 2 3 4 5 6 7 8 9 10

Connect the dots from **1** to **10**.

121

page 121

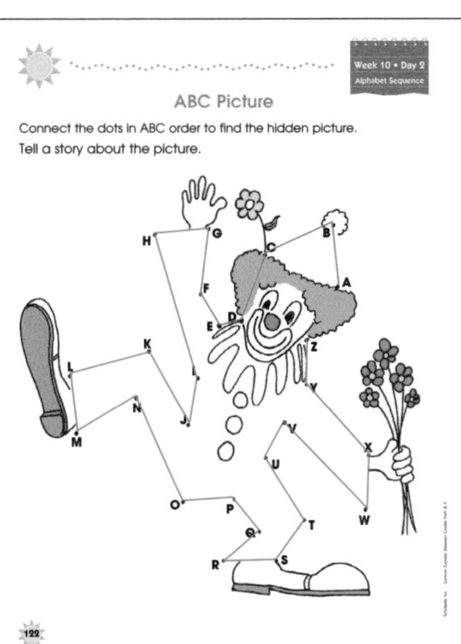

Week 10 • Day 2
Alphabet Sequence

ABC Picture

Connect the dots in ABC order to find the hidden picture.
Tell a story about the picture.

122

page 122

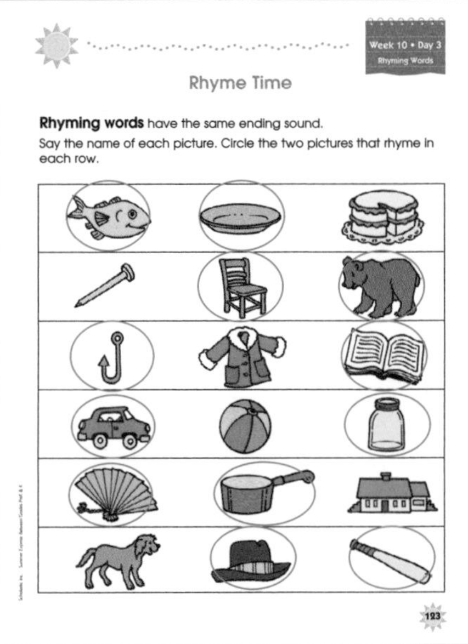

Week 10 • Day 3
Rhyming Words

Rhyme Time

Rhyming words have the same ending sound.
Say the name of each picture. Circle the two pictures that rhyme in each row.

123

page 123

Week 10 • Day 3
Rhyming Words

Check the Signs

Say the name of each picture. Circle the animal with the picture that rhymes with the first picture in each row.

124

page 124

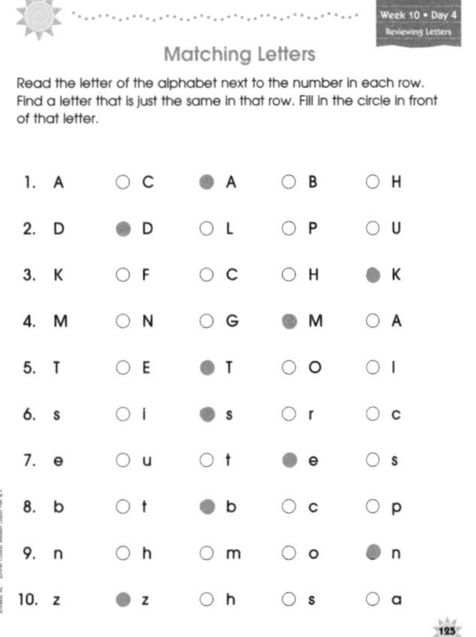

Week 10 • Day 4
Reviewing Letters

Matching Letters

Read the letter of the alphabet next to the number in each row. Find a letter that is just the same in that row. Fill in the circle in front of that letter.

1.	A	○ C	● A	○ B	○ H
2.	D	● D	○ L	○ P	○ U
3.	K	○ F	○ C	○ H	● K
4.	M	○ N	○ G	● M	○ A
5.	T	○ E	● T	○ O	○ I
6.	s	○ i	● s	○ r	○ c
7.	e	○ u	○ t	● e	○ s
8.	b	○ t	● b	○ c	○ p
9.	n	○ h	○ m	○ o	● n
10.	z	● z	○ h	○ s	○ a

125

page 125

Week 10 • Day 4
Review

Show What You Know

1. Which one is the same?
2. Which one is different?
3. Which animal name begins with the same sound?
4. Which animal name rhymes?

126

page 126

Picking Letters
Oh no! There they go!
8
1
I have A, B, C, and D.
2
I have U, V, W, and X, Y, Z.
7
I have Q, R, S, and T.
6
I have E, F, G, and H.
3
I have I, J, K, and L.
4
I have M, N, O, and P.
5

page 127

page 128

THIS CERTIFIES THAT

____

IS NOW READY

FOR GRADE ______

CONGRATULATIONS!

I'm proud of you! ____________________________

278443 PO# 400552